P9-CDE-878

Praise for
Disrupt Yourself
and Whitney Johnson

"Johnson, a Merrill Lynch equity analyst turned entrepreneur, shows how and why to upend a career in this practical, concise work. Savvy and often counterintuitive, this superb book offers the tools, mind-set guidance, and rationale for avoiding complacency and embracing a new career path."

—*Publishers Weekly*

"Playing it safe is not safe in today's fast-paced marketplace. *Disrupt Yourself* is a must-read for anyone looking to stand out from the crowd and pursue innovation in our highly uncertain business climate."

—Eric Ries, best-selling author of
The Lean Startup

"I have used the word 'disruption' to understand how some companies blossom while other wither. Whitney has applied the word in a different context – to understand why some individuals succeed in remarkable ways. Enjoyed this book!"

—Clayton M. Christensen,
Harvard Business School, *New York Times* best-selling author of *The Innovator's Dilemma*

"If you have gone through your career thinking that it is smarter and safer to 'stick with what you know,' get ready to have Whitney Johnson change your mind. Often what we already know can get in the way of what we don't know. *Disrupt Yourself* will inspire you to make the jump onto new learning curves, innovate, and stay at the top of your game."

—Liz Wiseman, best-selling author
of *Multipliers* and *Rookie Smarts*

"*Disrupt Yourself* reads like a handbook for innovation: it shows the incredible value of recognizing what you are good at and finding unexpected ways to apply those strengths to the marketplace. The dramatic 'jumps' that Johnson encourages us to take truly form the basis of creativity and success."

—Steve Wozniak, cofounder, Apple, Inc.
and chief scientist, Primary Data

"Too often we're told that to be successful in leadership or business, we must fit a certain mold. Whitney Johnson knows better. Applying the lessons of disruptive innovation to personal growth, she shows us how to pursue roles suited to our own strengths, to follow our own unique way of thinking and doing—and to dramatically increase our productivity, creativity, and happiness."

—Susan Cain, *New York Times* best-selling
author of *Quiet: The Power of Introverts
in a World that Can't Stop Talking*

"Wow! *Disrupt Yourself* wins the 'plain English' award—which is to say I've seldom if ever read a better written business/career development book. The advice is compelling, clear-as-a-bell, research-based, and actionable. And it'll work as well for a forty-something as a twenty-something."

—Tom Peters, best-selling author of
In Search of Excellence

"A motivating, compelling case for shifting gears right when we've reached our peaks. Whitney Johnson not only explains the why and how, but cheers us on along the way to greater meaning, learning, and innovation."

—Adam Grant, Wharton professor and
New York Times best-selling
author of *Give and Take*

"Leaders at all levels are often reminded that continuous learning and personal growth are key to successful careers and meaningful lives. In *Disrupt Yourself*, Whitney Johnson shows how to pursue them, purposefully building a foundation to keep oneself and others learning, changing, and thriving in the long term."

—Gianpiero Petriglieri, associate
professor of organizational behaviour,
INSEAD

"Whitney Johnson's *Disrupt Yourself* provides clear guidance that will help you both boost your career and become a driving force in market evolution. Her innovative approach proves that staying true to your own strengths can be groundbreaking, and often take you further than following established paths. I highly recommend this book."

—Michelle McKenna-Doyle,
SVP, CIO, National Football League

"You already know that to have the career—and life— you always wanted, you'll need to be innovative, take risks, and spot and seize opportunities. But how do you actually do any of those things? Because it's not at all obvious to most of us. Luckily, Whitney Johnson knows exactly how disruptive innovation gets done, and her brilliant new book *Disrupt Yourself* is the how-to guide you've been waiting for."

—Dr. Heidi Grant Halvorson, Columbia Business School, best-selling author of *Nine Things Successful People Do Differently* and *No One Understands You and What to Do About It*

Disrupt
Yourself

Disrupt Yourself

Putting the Power of *Disruptive Innovation* to Work

Whitney Johnson

Jefferson Madison
Regional Library
WITHDRAWN
Charlottesville, Virginia

bibliomotion
inc.

30736 R 4255

First published by Bibliomotion, Inc.
39 Harvard Street
Brookline, MA 02445
Tel: 617-934-2427
www.bibliomotion.com

Copyright © 2015 by Whitney Johnson

Disrupt Yourself is a registered trademark (TM) of
Whitney Johnson. All rights reserved.

All rights reserved. No part of this publication may be reproduced
in any manner whatsoever without written permission from the
publisher, except in the case of brief quotations embodied in critical
articles or reviews.

Printed in the United States of America

Library of Congress Cataloging-in-Publication Data

Johnson, Whitney (Whitney W.)
  Disrupt yourself : putting the power of disruptive innovation to work / Whitney
Johnson.
       pages cm
  Summary: "Disrupt Yourself will help people cope with the unpredictability of
disruption, and use it to their competitive advantage"—Provided by publisher.
  ISBN 978-1-62956-052-6 (hardback) — ISBN 978-1-62956-053-3 (ebook) — ISBN
978-1-62956-054-0 (enhanced ebook)
  1. Success in business. 2. Disruptive technologies. 3. Career changes. 4.
 Organizational change. 5. Strategic planning. I. Title.
  HF5386.J655 2015
  658.4'09—dc23
                                                                2015019271

To my husband,
who always says jump

Contents

Acknowledgments

Jodi Kantor of the *New York Times* once told me, "The first place I go in a book is to the Acknowledgments section."

Me too—so here goes.

To Clayton Christensen—thank you for the opportunity and privilege of working with and learning from you for nearly a decade—you inspired me to write this book.

Thank you to Jill Friedlander, Erika Heilman, Shevaun Betzler, Alicia Simons, Sue Ramin, and the entire Bibliomotion team for your professionalism: you are what every publisher should be. To my agent Josh Getzler, thank you for always giving advice in my best interest.

I owe a huge debt of gratitude to my long-time editor Amy Jameson at A+B Works. You are indispensable, alternatively editor, therapist, and cheerleader. To

Sarah Green, my editor at Harvard Business Review, I am continually in awe of your deft editorial touch. And thank you David Wan and Eric Hellweg for taking a chance on an unproven writer.

To Juan Carlos-Mendez, how I love to collaborate with you. Thank you for helping me apply the S-curve to personal disruption, and for the many ways in which you are smart that I am not. Stephanie Plamondon Bair, I so appreciative that you were willing to share your expertise in neuroscience; I still miss our walks around Fresh Pond.

Michaela Murphy, my speech coach, you have helped me find my voice. Laurel Christensen and Chrislyn Woolston at Time Out for Women, thank you for daring me to dig deeper. And a huge thanks to Amy Gray, my speaker's agent, for reminding every day that I have something to say.

To Brandon Jameson, I love the graphics that grace these pages. You always bring my ideas to life, better than I could have imagined. Macy Robison you continually find ways to showcase my ideas, beginning with my website, and are an unfailing friend. Becky Robinson, thanks for being so excited about evangelizing *Disrupt Yourself*—I love working with you. Meredith Fineman, you are a whiz at helping "do me, but better."

Thank you to old and new friends Carl Meacham, Heather Hunt, Brian Harker, and Connie Branyan; because of your review of early drafts, this book is much more readable.

To those who were willing to endorse this book, I am deeply indebted, and to the many readers of *Dare, Dream, Do,* thank you; you made this book possible.

Finally, to my husband, Roger, my children, David and Miranda, my many dear friends (you know who you are!), and to God, thank you for gently encouraging me to always, always, always show up.

Introduction

We're all equal before a wave.
—Laird Hamilton, professional surfer

In 2005, I was working as an equity analyst at Merrill Lynch. When one afternoon I told a close friend that I was going to leave Wall Street, she was dumbfounded. "Are you sure you know what you're doing?" she asked me. This was her polite, euphemistic way of wondering if I'd lost my mind.

My job was to issue buy or sell recommendations on corporate stocks—and I was at the top of my game. I had just returned from Mexico City for an investor day at America Movíl, now the fourth largest wireless operator in the world. As I sat in the audience with hundreds of others, Carlos Slim, the controlling shareholder and one of the world's richest men, quoted my research, referring to me as "La Whitney." I had large financial institutions like Fidelity Investments asking for my financial models, and when I upgraded or downgraded a stock, the stock price would frequently move several percentage points.

I was at the pinnacle of my Wall Street career, but getting to this place of power and respect had been hard won. My husband and I had moved to New York in 1989 so that he could pursue a PhD in molecular biology at Columbia University. While he was in school, we needed to pay our bills. I had to get a job. I'd majored in music (piano). I had no business credentials, connections, or confidence, so I started as a secretary to a retail sales broker at Smith Barney in midtown Manhattan. It was the era of *Liar's Poker, Bonfire of the Vanities,* and *Working Girl.* Working on Wall Street was exciting. I started taking business courses at night and I had a boss who believed in me, which allowed me to bridge from secretary to investment banker. This rarely happens. Later I became an equity research analyst and subsequently cofounded the investment firm Rose Park Advisors with Clayton Christensen, a professor at Harvard Business School.

When I walked onto Wall Street through the secretarial side door, and then walked off Wall Street to become an entrepreneur, I was a disruptor. "Disruptive innovation" is a term coined by Christensen to describe an innovation at the low end of the market that eventually upends an industry. In my case, I had started at the bottom and climbed to the top—now I wanted to upend my own career. No wonder my friend thought I'd lost my sanity.

According to Christensen's theory, disruptors secure

their initial foothold at the low end of the market, offering inferior, low-margin products. At first, the disruptor's position is weak. For example, when Toyota entered the U.S. market in the 1950s, it introduced the Corona, a small, cheap, no-frills car that appealed to first-time car buyers on a tight budget.

No one was worried about an upstart Japanese car manufacturer taking over a huge chunk of the American automobile market. In the theory of disruption, the market leader could have squashed this fledgling disruptor like a bug. But market leaders rarely bother. *It's a silly little product that would add nothing to the bottom line. Let's focus on bigger, faster, and better.* Early on, it didn't make sense for GM to defend against the Toyota Corona. The problem is that once a disruptor gains its footing, it too will be motivated to move upmarket, producing higher-quality, higher-margin products.[1] By the time a counterattack did make sense to GM, it was already too late. Toyota then moved happily upmarket with cars like the Camry and then the Lexus, eventually ceding the low end to Korea's Hyundai. Now, waiting in the low-end wings are India's Tata and China's Chery.

From Wall Street's perspective, these disruptors are the companies and people you want to invest in early on because their potential for growth is huge. Don't we all wish we had invested in Toyota back in the 70s?

But it's so easy to miss low-end disruptors.

I first started covering America Movíl, the Mexican telecom company, in 2002, building a financial model to determine whether the stock was over- or undervalued. To do this, I needed to predict how quickly wireless telephone adoption in Mexico would occur. In 2002, 25 percent of the Mexican population had adopted wireless, up from 1 percent just five years earlier, while standard landline penetration was about 15 percent. I now had to decide how much more wireless could grow. In analyzing who could afford a phone and who had access to credit, I thought wireless penetration could potentially reach 40 percent—or forty million people—by 2007.

Enter Carlos Slim, controlling shareholder of America Movíl. He saw a much bigger opportunity. In addition to the forty million people I saw, he saw the other sixty million people in Mexico who wanted to communicate but couldn't afford to. So what did Slim do? He offered subsidized handsets and prepaid cards, making credit a nonissue. Sound quality was poor, but bad sound was better than no sound. Over the next decade, landline penetration increased a paltry five percentage points, from 15 percent to 20 percent, while wireless penetration roared past my projection of 40 percent to 90 percent. And in the pursuit of profit, the technology got better. *That's* disruption.

When I first heard Clayton Christensen speak about disruption at an industry event, I recognized immediately that his theory explained why mobile penetration was repeatedly beating my estimates. Part of the reason disruption can be so hard to spot is the timing; the growth curve can look totally flat for years, then spike upward very steeply. In Mexico, wireless became available in 1988. For almost a decade, penetration was less than 1 percent, but in the five years between 1997 and 2002, penetration ramped to 25 percent.

As the pace of disruptive innovation quickens and you are in the midst of a crashing wave, what is unsettling can also be an amazing ride. This book isn't about simply *coping* with the force of disruption, but harnessing its power and unpredictability, learning to ride its waves, and to disrupt yourself.

You may be trying something new, like leaving an established career to become an entrepreneur, as I did when I left Wall Street. You may be changing jobs within your current industry or company, or jumping to an entirely new field. As you'll learn in the chapters that follow, disrupting yourself is critical to avoiding stagnation, being overtaken by low-end entrants (i.e., younger, smarter, faster workers), and fast-tracking your personal and career growth.

Understanding the S-Curve

Our view of the world is powered by personal algorithms. We observe how all of the components of our personal social system interact, looking for patterns to predict what will happen next. When systems behave linearly and react immediately, we tend to be fairly accurate with our forecasts. This is why toddlers love discovering light switches: cause and effect are immediate. But our predictive power plummets when there is a time delay or a nonlinear progression.

One of the best models for making sense of a non-linear world is the S-curve. This model has historically been used to understand how disruptive innovations take hold—why a growth curve will stay flat for so long and then rocket upward suddenly, only to eventually plateau again. Developed by E.M. Rogers in 1962, the S-curve model is an attempt to understand how, why, and at what rate ideas and products spread throughout cultures. Adoption is relatively slow at first, at the base of the S, until a tipping point, or knee of the curve, is reached. You then move into hyper-growth, up the sleek, steep back of the curve. This is usually at somewhere between 10 to 15 percent of market penetration. At the flat part at the top of the S, you've reached saturation, typically at 90 percent.

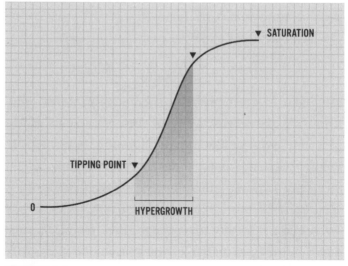

FIGURE 1-1

Facebook, for example, based on a market opportunity of one billion users, took roughly four years to reach penetration of 10 percent. But once Facebook reached a critical mass of a hundred million users, rapid growth ensued due to the network effect (i.e., friends and family were now on Facebook), as well as virality (e-mail updates, photo albums for friends of friends, etc.); over the next four years, Facebook added not one hundred million but eight hundred million users.[2]

I believe the S-curve can also be used to understand personal disruption—the necessary pivots in our own career paths. In complex systems like a business or a brain, cause and effect may not always be as clear as the relationship between the light switch and the lightbulb. There are time-delayed and time-dependent relationships in which huge effort may yield little in the near term, or in which high output today may be the result of actions taken a long time ago. The S-curve decodes these patterns, providing signposts along a path that, while frequently trodden, is not always obvious. If you can successfully navigate, even harness, the successive cycles of learning and mastering that resemble the S-curve model, you will see and seize opportunities in an era of accelerating disruption.

Self-disruption will force you up steep foothills of new information, relationships, and systems. The looming mountain may seem insurmountable, but the S-curve helps us understand that if we keep working at it, we can reach that inflection point where our understanding and competence will suddenly shoot upward. This is the fun part of disruption, rapidly scaling to new heights of success and achievement. Eventually, you will plateau and your growth will taper off. Then it's time to look for new ways to disrupt.

One story that shows how the S-curve model can help us better forecast the future is the experience of golfer Dan McLaughlin. Never having played eighteen holes of golf, McLaughlin quit his job as a commercial photographer in April 2010 to pursue a goal of becoming a top professional golfer through ten thousand hours of deliberate practice. During the first eighteen months, improvement was slow as McLaughlin practiced his putting, chipping, and drive. Then, as he began to put the various pieces together, he moved into a phase of dizzying growth. Within five years, he had surpassed 96 percent of the twenty-six million golfers who register a handicap with the US Golf Association (USGA). Though McLaughlin was keen to move from the top 4 percent to the top 1 percent of amateur golfers, as he achieved mastery, S-curve math predicted his rate of improvement would decline more and more sharply over time.

The Psychology of Disruption

The S-curve also helps us understand the psychology of disrupting ourselves. As we launch into something new, understanding that progress may at first be almost imperceptible helps keep discouragement at bay. It also helps us recognize why the steep part of the learning curve is so fun. When you are learning, you are feeling the effects of dopamine, a neurotransmitter in your brain that makes you feel good. It's an office dweller's version of thrill seeking. Once we reach the upper flat portion of the S-curve and things become habitual or automatic, our brains create less of these feel-good chemicals and boredom can kick in, making an emotional case for personal disruption. At a career peak, there is certainly the specter of competition from below, but just as importantly, there's the risk that if we aren't on a curve that satisfies us emotionally, we may be the cause of our own undoing. When we are no longer getting an emotional reward from our career, we may actually end up doing our job poorly.

With learning, our progress doesn't follow a straight

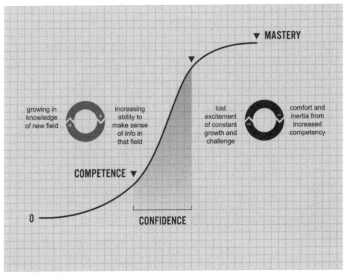

FIGURE 1-2

line. It is exponential and expands by multiples. Instead of learning a fixed number of facts and figures each day, what we learn is proportional to what we've already learned. We needn't merely plod along, moving one up and one over on the graph paper of existence. If we apply the right variables, we can explode into our own mastery.

I've identified seven variables that can speed up or slow down the movement of individuals or organizations along the curve, including:

Taking the right risks
Playing to your distinctive strengths
Embracing constraints
Battling entitlement
Stepping back to grow
Giving failure its due
Being discovery driven

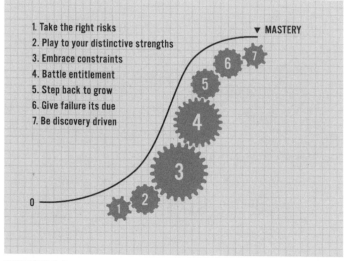

FIGURE 1-3

We'll devote a chapter to each.

This book is about surfing the S-curves of your own personal disruption. Yes, disruption can feel a bit scary, but the payoff of career growth and personal achievement makes overcoming the fear factor well worth it. We all start at the low end of the learning curve. This book will teach you how to shift into hypergrowth and, when your learning crests, to do what great disruptors do: catch a new wave.

1

Take the Right Risks

*Be a Columbus to whole new continents and
worlds within you, opening new channels,
not of trade, but of thoughts.*
—Henry David Thoreau

You're trying something new: you've made a lateral move, been promoted, or started a new job. You are confident that you can be successful, but so much is unfamiliar. It's easy to become frustrated. Take a deep breath, and remember that at the beginning of this S-shaped growth curve, progress will be slow.

Very little is habitual at the low end of a learning curve. Considerable effort may seem to yield few results. Mapping new mental territory and creating new neuronal and electrochemical connections take time.[1] But, as you practice, new neural networks are formed, and stimulating one neuron in a sequence stimulates others. The basal ganglia, an oval of brain cells about the size of an apricot, bursts with activity, analyzing everything—every interaction with stakeholders, every piece of data—and begins to detect patterns. To maximize efficiency, the human brain converts these patterns or sequences of actions into a routine known as "chunking." For instance, I'm guessing that you simply "brush your teeth" without breaking that task down into disparate parts like reaching for the tube of toothpaste, picking it up, unscrewing the cap, and so on. The more chunking occurs, the more reflexive an activity becomes.[2]

But if a task is not both meaningful and relevant, your brain will have little motivation to learn it—and thus to move up the S-curve. Therefore, the first thing you need to ask is, "What is it that I am trying to accomplish?" Or, in other words: What job needs to be done?

Understanding the Job-to-Be-Done

The Merriam-Webster dictionary definition of "to hire" is "to give work to a person in exchange for wages or payment". But "hiring" can have a much broader definition, extending to every product and service we use. Whenever we buy something, we are "hiring" that product or service to take care of an unmet need, to do a "job." This is an essential part of the outcome-driven innovation process introduced by Anthony Ulwick[3] and popularized by Clayton

Christensen, who calls it the "jobs-to-be-done" theory. To develop a new service or bring a new product to market, an innovator applying this theory doesn't focus on a customer's age or gender. Instead, she focuses on what problem the customer needs solved, and who or what can be hired to do that job.

Every job that people want done, with few exceptions, has both functional and emotional elements. Take, for example, buying a home. There is an obvious unmet need—putting a roof over your head. However, if you buy a larger house than you require for shelter or spend hours planting a garden in the backyard, there's also an emotional job afoot.

Consider your use of social media. Perhaps you, like me, hire Twitter to help you expand your network. JP Rangaswami, chief data officer for Deutsche Bank, described tweets as the "knowledge worker's pheromones,"[4] a means of sending signals to others. I also hire Twitter to prototype my ideas in real time and to learn to think more concisely. Now that LinkedIn has added a publishing platform, I can hire it to help me hone my personal voice via blog posts, in addition to consulting its repository of résumés when I am on the hunt for talent. Because the list of jobs that Linked-In can do for me has expanded, like an all-purpose cleaner, I seem to hire LinkedIn at least once a day.

As a professional investor, I hire an investment to do the functional job of making money. But whether I realize it or not, I am also hiring the investment to do an emotional job for me. To illustrate my point, let's take a look at the U.S. reality show *Shark Tank*, which features budding entrepreneurs presenting their business plans to five self-made multimillionaires, hoping to convince them to invest. During the second episode of season 6, Mark Cuban invested in a company called Roominate, an award-winning line of toys designed to inspire innovators, founded by two female engineers out of Stanford and MIT.[5] One of Cuban's conditions was that the founders mentor his two young daughters. In addition to a financial return, he was looking for an emotional return for himself, and an educational return for his children.[6]

Identifying the Job You Want Done

When you are beginning a new project, you need to figure out what "jobs"—both functional and emotional—this new endeavor will do for you. It's best to clarify this either before you switch to a new role or as soon as possible thereafter. As executive coach Pam Fox Rollin shares in her book *42 Rules for Your New Leadership Role,* "Many flameouts can be traced to missteps during [the] first quarter...[F]or the 60–75% of leaders that survive into a second year (one third fail within the first year), their effectiveness and trajectory are powerfully affected by choices made in the first year."[7] To make better choices early on, take the time to figure out why you're really making a move.

For a concrete way of thinking about this, I always

come back to a lecture given by Steve Kaufman, former CEO of Arrow Electronics, at Harvard Business School in 2010. Like job role changes, corporate mergers are a time of transition—and hence anxiety. Kaufman recounted advice from the former head of Arrow's acquisition integration team, Betty Jane Hess: "When we make an acquisition, every employee has just three questions: (1) Do I have a job? (2) Who do I report to? And (3) How will I get paid? Until they get answers, nothing else matters." Let's take each in turn:

1. **Do I have a job?** In psychologist Abraham Maslow's hierarchy of needs, one of the most basic is to feel secure. But once we've got the paycheck that will put food in our stomachs and shelter over our heads, we need to feel that we belong, that what we do matters,[8] and that we are learning. These are needs not often covered by our formal job descriptions. Similarly, our companies and coworkers need things from us that go beyond our job titles. If you're a producer at an ad agency, your job is ostensibly to bring marketing assets to life. If you're a computer programmer, your job is to write code. But perhaps it's also your job to do the emotional work of achieving consensus among stakeholders, or the logistical job of keeping people on track. For the person who says, "I just want to do my (functional) job," the realization that he will not be rewarded solely on his domain expertise can come as a shock. When people decide to make a change, it's

often because the work no longer does the emotional job they originally hired it to do, or because they want to shed some of the unspoken "jobs" that came with the role. So when you're planning a move, be very clear on what the job is, from the company's perspective and yours, both functionally and emotionally.

2. **Who do I report to?** If you've been through a merger, you know just how blurry the reporting structure can be. But uncertainty can be found in any work situation, not just after a takeover. When people don't know to whom they answer, or the metrics by which they will be measured, there will be chaos.

Research from Colin Camerer, a neuroscientist at Caltech, and his colleagues indicates that people prefer known risks to ambiguity. When test subjects were asked to make decisions based on little or ambiguous information, they exhibited substantially more activity in the amygdala, an area of the brain associated with fear, than when they were asked to make decisions they *knew* were risky. It's this inexplicable fright—an irrational by-product of not knowing—that keeps us from focusing on the possibility of future rewards.[9] Once you solve the problem of where you fit, to whom you'll be accountable, and how your contributions will be measured, your brain can spend less time worrying and more time learning.

3. **How will I get paid?** Notice that the question here is not *how much*. We all want to be paid in cold

hard cash, and preferably a good amount of it. That's the functional reason people work. But how else will you be compensated? What about the emotional rewards that are worth far more to most people than dollars and cents? Wouldn't you stay at a job longer because of intangibles such as long-term opportunities, the belief that you are building something important, or the feeling that you have a seat at the table? Are you more motivated by pride (seeing your name on the brass plaque) or by gratitude (hearing a customer say "thank you")? By problem solving or by praise? You can't go after the rewards that matter to you—or properly reward your colleagues—if you don't first know what those rewards are.

This is probably a good time to answer that lingering question my friend, my husband, and probably you, had: *why did you walk away from Wall Street?* Knowing that work does a functional and emotional job, the logic becomes clear. I was at a point where I could continue to hire Merrill Lynch to pay the bills, but I could no longer hire it for the emotional rewards. Not only had I reached the top of a learning curve with no prospects for jumping to a new one because management liked me 'right where I was,' I discovered that notwithstanding performance metrics that were 20% better than my peers, we all received the same bonus. The emotional cost of staying had become too high when I could no longer bring my dreams to work.[10]

Nature Favors Risk Takers

Starting something new means taking a risk. But in our society, the word "risk" has assumed mostly negative connotations. When someone tells us "that's risky," most of us have a visceral, fearful reaction. But Mother Nature seems to have built a loophole into our sense of well-being, because embedded somewhere within the human genetic makeup is an inclination to take risks.

Of course, in order for evolution and natural selection to favor risk-taking as a behavior there has to be a benefit, and that benefit has to outweigh the outcome of doing nothing. Many examples from the animal kingdom support this hypothesis. According to research by Dr. Lee Alan Dugatkin, who was trying to understand a continuum of risk-taking, fish willing to take risks were likely to mate better.[11]

Guppies, for example, engage in what is known as predator inspection behavior. Predator inspection is akin to guard duty. A few fish break away from the group and slowly approach the predator to obtain information. In taking risks in the presence of a predator, a guppy is more likely to get eaten, but a male guppy that takes this risk is more attractive as a mate to females.[12] The bolder guppies are also better at learning.

Fortune may favor the brave guppy, but what if you aren't a risk-taker by nature? According to psychologists Tory Higgins and Heidi Grant Halvorson, people can be divided into two personality categories: those who are promotion focused and those who are prevention focused.[13] Those whose motivation is promotion focused are comfortable taking chances, like to work quickly, dream big, and think creatively: they are natural risk-takers, focused on maximizing gain. In contrast, people who are prevention focused tend to concentrate on staying safe, work slowly and meticulously, worry what might go wrong if they aren't careful enough, and focus on preserving what they have.

So for the risk averse who are trying to convince themselves to try something new, the trick is not to focus on what will be gained by venturing forth, but to instead focus on what might be lost by standing still. For example, if I'm a really prevention-focused person thinking about asking for a promotion, I shouldn't try to psych myself up for it by imagining all the accolades I might win or the new projects I might take on. I should focus on what I might miss out on—the great projects I might not get assigned to, or the money I'm leaving on the table.

Identify the Right Risks

As you gear yourself up to take risks, it's also important to distinguish between *competitive* risk and *market* risk.

Competitive. If a colleague comes to you, and says, "The opportunity for this product is huge and I've got the projections to prove it," it's quite likely that a competing company or individual has scoped out the opportunity. There's probably already a kingpin. It's not you. You can be confident there will be customers for your product or service, but you have to assess whether you can compete and win. This is competitive risk.

Market. If instead your colleague says, "I don't know if there's a market, but I think there's a need not being met," you are looking at market risk. You have no idea if there will be customers for your product or idea, so a forecast of what you might earn in the future is fiction. However, if you can find customers who want to hire your product, as the first mover you are favored to own the market.

Because our brains make a mountain out of a molehill of uncertainty, we tend to prefer competitive risk because it *feels* more secure. But the empirical evidence says that market risk is less risky than competitive risk.[14]

The classic example is Clayton Christensen's analysis of the disk drive industry. He divided the eighty-plus firms that entered the disk drive industry from 1976 to 1993 into two major categories: firms that sought growth through a disruptive strategy, introducing a new product and creating a market for that product (market risk), and companies that pursued growth with proven technologies in established markets (competitive risk). Of the fifty-two firms that entered established markets, only three (6 percent) ever reached $100 million in revenue. In contrast, of the thirty-two firms that entered a market that was less than two years old, twelve (37 percent) surpassed $100 million in revenue. In addition, the firms that created new markets logged $62 billion in accumulated revenue between 1976 and 1994, compared with $3.3 billion for those that moved into established markets. Based on this research, when you take on market versus competitive risk, the odds of success are six times (37 percent versus 6 percent) higher and the revenue opportunity twenty times greater.[15]

Another hack for helping your brain reconsider market risk is to take a look at stock market valuations. In analyzing forty companies that were identified as disruptive (i.e., took on market risk) in the ten years after they went public, the average price/earnings multiple for these stocks was 30x, or double that of the broader market. Because this basket of stocks initially looked overvalued, one could understandably argue that competitive risk is a safer bet. However, when the high price of these disruptors was compared to their much higher growth rate, these stocks didn't look so pricey. Relative to companies that were taking on competitive risk these disruptors looked expensive, but relative to their own growth rate (which was initially underestimated because the market had yet to be created) the stocks were actually a bargain.[16] In other words, market risk is the right kind of risk when you're looking for a new learning curve to scale.

Here's another way to think about it. When I evaluate an investment, one of the first questions I ask is: "Is this company flying under the radar?" Meaning, is it unattractive enough that competitors have no incentive to either co-opt it or gun it down? It's better to be treated as a paper airplane than a fighter jet. When you are disrupting, the best possible start-up scenario is to be dismissed, even ignored, just as Blockbuster ignored Netflix—right up until Blockbuster was "netflixed."[17]

Southern New Hampshire University (SNHU) is a good example of an organization that took on fly-under-the-radar market risk.[18] A decade ago, SNHU was a two-thousand-student college with declining enrollment. Instead of trying to increase enrollment by competing for Ivy League–caliber professors at the high end or with government-funded community colleges at the low end, the university chose to play where no one else was playing—online. There was no guarantee that students would be interested in online degree programs. But because SNHU took on market risk, playing where no one else was playing, and there were many students looking for the flexibility provided by online courses, it is now considered the Amazon of education, with thirty-four thousand students enrolled. SNHU is in the process of jumping to yet another growth curve to decrease the cost of a college degree by measuring competencies rather than credits. One student demonstrated all

120 competencies in one hundred days. His associate's degree cost a grand total of $1,250.

A good example of taking on market risk in personal, career terms is Amy Jo Martin, founder of Digital Royalty. In 2008, of the hundreds of millions of dollars being spent on advertising and publicity by the NBA, very little was allocated to social media. Martin saw an unmet need, and leveraged her expertise to persuade the Phoenix Suns to hire her as director of digital media, a first-of-its-kind position within the NBA. Martin's clients have included Shaquille O'Neal, and she has more than a million Twitter followers. Her gig sounds fantastically fun, but at the outset people wondered if it was even a job.

Avoid the Wrong Risks

In 1996, when I was working for Smith Barney, I moved from banking to equity research, having been hired to cover the cement and construction sector in Latin America. Within weeks of my move, Smith Barney bought Salomon Brothers, and Salomon Brothers already had a highly regarded *Institutional Investor*-ranked analyst in cement and construction. Rather than knocking on a door that was closed, I opened a window: there were a number of media companies going public with no analyst to follow them, so I volunteered for that beat. Rather than trying to outcompete the incumbent construction analyst, I took on market risk, as disruption theory would dictate. Of course, it was a lot messier and more painful than the narrative makes it sound, but within a year I also was an *Institutional Investor*-ranked analyst. By venturing into an unmarked market with few competitors, I was able to scale this new curve quickly.

A classic mistake made during venture capital booms is to fund start-ups that have good ideas but no staying power because an established player will have the incentive to co-opt the idea and squash the up-and-comer like a bug. TIVo, for example, was co-opted by cable and telecom companies that poured millions of dollars into embedding digital video recorders into their set-top boxes, making TIVo hardware redundant. TomTom GPS was a great idea until GPS functionality was built into smartphones. These brilliant new ideas became services that are now broadly offered, but the firms that started developing them have ceased to exist as independent entities. Competitive risk cancelled their climb up the S-curve of disruption.

Here's what that this scenario can look like for an individual: one firm I've consulted with had hired a new portfolio manager to make investment decisions for the firm. There was a senior person on staff who thought that was *his* job. To succeed, the new hire needed the senior staffer to cooperate. But the senior staffer saw the new hire as an interloper. It turned into a game of chicken. The senior staffer was eventually let go, but the new hire suffered a huge loss of political capital early on as he competed with an established employee to accomplish the same job.

Brain science also supports market risk over competitive risk. The stressed out, "on-guard" or fearful state of mind associated with competition wears down our cognitive functioning over time. When you compete, it's as if you are going into battle. Your sympathetic nervous system mobilizes the body for a fight-or-flight response, activating the hypothalamus, stimulating the pituitary gland, and releasing cortisol. Your body likes the cortisol initially. This is why studies have found that soldiers in combat are more effective their first month on the front lines. But as that cortisol rush levels off, cognitive functioning deteriorates. Judgment, memory, and even the immune system all decline, while irritability, depression, moodiness, and gastrointestinal ailments increase.[19]

Taking a market risk involves a much healthier mental state. In my own experience, even though I crave certainty and the control of a focused task to complete, moving into terra incognita feels better. It is restorative, both emotionally and physically. A study done by Kennon M. Sheldon and colleagues suggests that opportunities for self-expression—for example, creativity—may increase feelings of agreeableness, conscientiousness and openness, leading people to act more responsibly, cooperatively, receptively, and cheerfully.[20] While we perceive a new-fangled idea as more risky than an established one, what happens in our brains tells us otherwise.

Identify a Job No One Else Can Do

For real staying power, it's important to specialize in such a way that there is no one else doing the job.[21] A few summers ago, my friend's eleven-year-old triplets wanted to earn some money. They set up a lemonade stand. Instead of setting up in front of the house, like kids usually do, they set up next to a high school football field after practice on a hot summer day. There was no guarantee there would be a market for the lemonade at the football field. But there was no competition either. If there were customers, the entire market was going to be theirs for the taking. It was. These eleven-year-olds earned $75 in about twenty minutes.

You'll know you're dealing with market risk when you realize there is no one else doing a job that needs to be done. Rachael Chong saw social good organizations recruiting skilled volunteers but then doing little except asking them to give money or directing them to do mind-numbing tasks like stuff envelopes. Chong came up with a plan to templatize the various functions of a nonprofit so that professionals could actually donate their expertise, not just their time and money. A marketer may help a nonprofit rebrand its website, while an HR person helps a social enterprise set up a time-off policy. In just five years, Chong's company, Catchafire, had more than five thousand social good organizations as clients, more than twenty thousand skilled volunteers, and was one of the largest talent providers for nonprofits in the world.

When you make the decision to start something new, first figure out the jobs you want to do. Then position yourself to play where no one else is playing. Despite our love affair with the certainty of competitive risk, the natural world, business research, and brain science all tell us that trying something new is less risky and ultimately more satisfying. It's the difference between a friends-and-family lemonade stand that earns a few dollars and one that takes in multiples of that—because customers are truly thirsty for what you know how to do, and because you're the only one serving it up.

2

Play to Your Distinctive Strengths

Each bird must sing with its own throat.
—Henrik Ibsen

Disruptors not only look for unmet needs, they match those needs with their distinctive strengths. A distinctive strength is something that you do well that others within your sphere don't. Pairing this strength with a need to be met or problem to be solved gives you the momentum necessary to move into hypergrowth, the sweet spot of the S-curve. In this chapter, we'll review what a distinctive strength is, talk about how to identify yours, match them with unmet needs, and then explore how this pairing allows you to accelerate up the curve.

In nature, it is abundantly clear that playing to distinctive strengths is what provides sustenance and allows an organism to thrive. I am stunned by the incredible diversity that exists within the animal kingdom, for example. Each organism has evolved to exploit a specific niche or adapt to a different climate.

Sometimes the strength is specific and obvious. Think about the cuddly little koala, sleeping up to twenty hours a day. One might have serious doubts about its ability to survive. However, the koala can do something that almost no other animal can: it uses eucalyptus leaves, which have minimal nutritional and caloric value, as a food source.

Sometimes the strength will be less obvious. Consider Charles Darwin's finches, a subject you may vaguely remember from high school biology class. When Darwin first encountered these birds on the Galapagos Islands, he gathered numerous specimens, not quite realizing what he had discovered. Upon his return, he presented these specimens to the famous English ornithologist John Gould for identification. Gould's analysis revealed that the specimens Darwin had submitted were in fact highly variable. What at first glance were all just "finches" turned out to be twelve different species. There were similarities, but evolution had allowed each to develop a distinctive strength. Each species had a novel beak structure that allowed it to exploit a specific food resource. Some evolved to eat seeds, others fruit, others insects, and others grubs. In business terms, they all had similar core competencies (feathers, wings, feet, beak), but it was a distinctive, seemingly subtle strength—the *type* of beak—that allowed the finches to effectively compete for a specific type of food.

Identify What You Do Well

What are you good at? Do you have an obvious advantage like the koala, or will you need to do a little hunting like Darwin's finches? The following list of questions is not exhaustive, but it will get you started:

1. **What skills have helped you survive?** Like the finches whose beaks are adapted for the birds' survival, you have skills you've developed out of necessity.

Scott Edinger is a highly successful consultant and CEO advisor—a role he could not have conceived of in his youth. He never knew his father, grew up broke and living in a trailer park, and at age nine, his mother left and he was adopted into less than ideal circumstances. Scott learned to survive his challenging childhood by becoming an expert in communication, conflict resolution, attunement to others, and raw persuasion. In college he put the paint and polish on his communication skills, placing in the top five in over a hundred debate tournaments, and earning bronze medals at the national championships, while completing a bachelor of science in communication and rhetoric.

Fast forward: prior to starting his own consulting firm, Edinger was an Executive Vice President of Sales, and has been globally ranked #2 in sales in a division of a Fortune 500 company. He is the author of two books and a contributor to the Harvard Business Review, for which he wrote a popular and often-quoted magazine article, "How to Make Yourself Indispensable." As a consultant, he has repeatedly helped Fortune 500 companies turn around under-performing divisions by focusing on a critical survival skill in business – how to sell.

What unique skills have you developed to survive and then applied within your career to thrive?

2. **What makes you feel strong?** Marcus Buckingham, the author of *Now, Discover Your Strengths*, explains: "Our strengths...clamor for attention in the most basic way: using them makes you feel strong. Take note of the times when you feel invigorated, inquisitive, successful...these moments are clues to what your strengths are."[1] If you identify and focus on what makes you feel strong, you can also expect to be happier, which, according to researchers, "leads to more flexible and adaptive thinking and to enhanced innovative ability and problem solving in a wide range of circumstances."[2]

Do you feel strong when you're teaching or learning, when you're buying or selling, when you're leading a team or creating on your own?

3. **What exasperates you about others?** When I wrote about this topic for *Harvard Business Review*, reader Alana Cates pointed out another way of

identifying our hidden strengths: "When are you exasperated? The frustration of genius is in believing that if it is easy for you, it must be easy for everyone else."[3] Whether you are an engineer, musician, scientist, or professor struggling to manage the work of subordinates or peers, it may not be that they're deficient, just that you're unusually skilled.

Where does your "genius" emerge?

4. What made you different, even an oddball, as a child? As children we do what we love to do—even if that makes us an oddity. When you look back to childhood passions, you are likely to discover an innate talent.

In elementary school, Candice Brown Elliott's classmates teasingly called her "Encyclopedia Brown" after the character in the children's books. She recounts, "All the kids thought I was the smartest kid in school, but most of my teachers were deeply frustrated with me, because I got only average grades. I was labeled an *underachiever.*" She found schoolwork boring, so she didn't pay attention. Instead, she says, "I daydreamed of having animated conversations with famous people like Madame Curie or Benjamin Franklin. I daydreamed about building the first true Artificial Intelligence (AI) that would reside in my bedroom closet. I daydreamed about how to build floating cities, great inventions, and new forms of art."

High school was a similar experience; Elliott was reading two or three novels a week, but she flunked

English class because she didn't want to participate in dissecting literature that was "trashy and juvenile." The second semester she was placed in "Survival English," the school mistakenly taking her failing grade as evidence that she couldn't read.

Despite not doing her schoolwork, Elliott continued to ace her exams and was muddling through with a C average. "Senior year, one instructor cornered me in the hallway angrily demanding to know why I never did the work. I replied, 'It interferes with my studies.' Thinking that I was being a smart-aleck kid, he angrily asked what I was studying... so I told him. He was dumbfounded that I was self-studying at an advanced university level, using my father's university textbooks, among others. He then challenged me and said, 'I want you to take my third semester Chem AP class.' To which I objected, 'But I haven't taken the first two semesters.' He overcame my objection by informing me that the third semester was by invitation only, would have only five students, and we each had to do only one semester project, of our own choosing. That final semester I had the same teacher for both Chem AP and English." Elliott was on the honor roll that final semester, earning straight As.

Four decades later, Candice Brown Elliott holds ninety U.S.-issued patents. Her most famous invention, PenTile, color flat-panel display architecture, is shipping in hundreds of millions of smartphones, tablets, notebook PCs, and high-resolution televisions. She founded a venture-backed company to develop this technology, and later sold it to Samsung. She says, "If you see me at my desk, you'll likely catch me daydreaming still."

As a child, Elliott's daydreaming was considered odd by her classmates and tremendously frustrating by her teachers. As an adult, her daydreaming, autodidactic approach is her superpower.

Is there something that made you peculiar when you were young? Could it be your superpower?

5. **What compliments do you shrug off?** All too frequently, we are oblivious to our own strengths. The trouble with certain strengths is that you do them so reflexively well they can be easy to overlook.

Perhaps you've had an experience similar to that of Neil Reay, managing director at Cancer Treatment Centers of America. When he asked for recommendations on his LinkedIn profile, he discovered, "Several things that others said about my strengths were not the things I was using as 'Core Skills' in my own profile, but were valuable to those around me."[4]

Keep an eye out for those compliments you habitually dismiss not because you are being coy, but because this "thing" feels as natural as breathing. It may even be you've heard a compliment so many times, you are sick of it! Why can't people praise you for the thing that you've worked really, really hard to do well?

A great example is Viniece Jennings, a senior fellow in the Environmental Leadership Program. After taking Gallup's StrengthsFinder survey, she discovered that she was socially outgoing, reliable, genuine, and authentic. She was happy to learn that she was considered emotionally intelligent, but her type A alter ego was disappointed that qualities such as strategic, analytical, or focused weren't in her lineup. Wondering if the survey was somehow incomplete, she asked friends and colleagues about the results. They responded, "Yep, that's you" or, "That quality really sets you apart." Because she has a PhD in environmental science and works as a research scientist, Jennings shares, "I expected to be mechanically analytical, inquisitive about everything environmental, and perhaps walking around with a statistics book."

Given the seeming disconnect between her perceived strengths and the test results, Jennings looked to her past for proof of her supposed emotional intelligence. She'd grown up in Athens, Georgia, where there are a lot of landfills. After starting college in Delaware, she discovered that trash from Delaware was frequently routed to Georgia. She says, "On campus, every time I saw someone waste something I was sick inside because I knew it might be shipped to my hometown." That's when she wrote a mini-grant and managed a campus-wide recycling program in her spare time. A college friend recently sent her a picture of the new recycling bins at her alma mater, with the text "all because of you." Remembering the impact of this experience, Jennings could see just how powerful and important her empathic strengths are, and that these strengths are a distinctive advantage within her chosen field of environmental science.

The tendency to deflect compliments around what we do reflexively well is understandable, perhaps even justifiable, but over the course of a career (or the life of a company), it will leave us trading at a discount to what we are really worth. Nineteenth-century essayist Ralph Waldo Emerson wrote: "In every work of genius we recognize our own rejected thoughts; they come back to us with a certain alienated majesty." Don't assume that just because something comes easily or seems obvious to you, it's not rare and valuable to someone else.

What compliments do you repeatedly dismiss?

6. **What are your hard-won skills?** These proficiencies aren't necessarily your best skills, but typically they carry a price tag of sweat and possibly tears, and they speak volumes about you. These are the skills you point to when someone asks, "What is the hardest thing you've ever done?" While I was at Merrill Lynch, a résumé came across my desk for a fellow straight out of undergrad named Rob Larson. I liked that he'd majored in math, but what made him an especially attractive candidate for investment banking was that he'd earned money for college as a cowhand. We interviewed him; Goldman Sachs hired him. In a competitive field of candidates, his résumé stood out, not because herding cattle was a requisite skill for the job, but because he was no stranger to hard work.

Hard-won skills not only signal an ability to stick with a difficult task, they are often "pay-to-play" skills, a hurdle you have to jump to be able to do the job, and are thus vital at the outset of a career or upon reentry to the workforce after an extended leave of absence. Early in my professional life, it was apparent that if I wanted to play in the Wall Street sandbox, I had to pay by learning financial analysis, coursework not covered in my liberal arts curriculum. In almost every industry there are pay-to-play skills. When you muscle your way to acquiring these, they'll give you the heft you need to scale existing curves and jump to new ones.

What skills have you worked really hard to obtain?

Identify Your Distinctive Strengths

Once you've identified your underlying assets or your core strengths, you also need to spot your distinctive strengths, defined as what you do well that others in your sphere don't, in order to set your hand- and footholds along the curve.

Here's an example: in the film *The Hundred-Foot Journey*, the Kadam family has sought asylum in Europe due to election disputes in Mumbai, India. After an initial stay in England, they make their way to a small village in France on the border of Switzerland. The father purchases an abandoned restaurant across the street—a hundred feet away—from an upscale French restaurant. Much of the humor in the film is about the rivalry between the two restaurateurs.

What is interesting from the perspective of disruption is following the learning curve of Hassan, the second-oldest son. He is a talented chef whose specialty is, not surprisingly, Indian cooking. But to gain stature as a chef, Hassan must master the French tradition. Only once he's mastered the pay-to-play skill of French cuisine can he infuse it with Indian spices and flavors. This French–Indian fusion is his distinctive strength (what he does well that others within his sphere don't) and wins him the industry's coveted Michelin star.

For a real-life example, consider the story of industrial designer Adam Richardson. At age six, he was sketching designs for cars; by age nine, he was surveying neighbors about their driving habits and measuring their car interiors. Thirty years ago, this was a unique strength—no one was approaching design through the lens of research. When Richardson graduated from college, because he hadn't yet keyed in on this strength, he took a fairly traditional industrial designer job at Sun Microsystems. He quickly realized that most of his design industry colleagues were brilliantly creative but not particularly attuned to customers' needs. He, by contrast, wasn't the strongest stylist but was enthralled with market research and good at capturing it.

"I'm a good listener, and I like finding patterns in chaotic qualitative data," he explains. He looked for a graduate program to help him hone those skills, but because popular ones like that at the Illinois Institute of Technology (IIT) and Stanford Design Program didn't exist then, he ended up cobbling together a course for himself via the University of Chicago's self-directed Master of Arts Program in the Humanities. Once Richardson was willing to veer from the traditional industrial design path to study anthropology, ethnography, sociology, cultural theory, and art history, he was able to make the leap to a dream job at design consultancy Frog. He is now a financial services disruptor at Financial Engines.[5]

Lieutenant Joseph "DuckDuck" Geeseman planned on teaching neuroscience at the college level, but when he graduated the job market was abysmal. So he started looking for an unmet need outside of academia. He applied to Facebook and Google (to possibly work with their data algorithms), to Hershey's and Kraft (to be a food scientist), and to casino game companies (to make algorithms and stimuli that would keep people playing longer). Because his mother was an army officer he also applied to the military.

It turns out the military was interested in his PhD in neuroscience; the United States Navy has more than thirty active duty aerospace psychologists. Now that he has obtained the pay-to-play skill of basic flight training, Lt. Geeseman's expertise in neuroscience and psychology is a distinctive strength as he designs aircraft and pilot interfaces. And he gets to do more science and research than he could have imagined.

Match Your Strengths with Unmet Needs

Once you have a clear picture of your one-of-a-kind skills, you can match those skills to unmet needs. Consider jobs where you'd be the wild-card candidate. Or look for ways to combine your passions. Look at problems that the organization needs solved, and ask yourself: Can I fix that?

When Jayne Juvan, a partner at the law firm Roetzel & Andress in Cleveland, Ohio, started using social media, very, very few lawyers used these tools. Because her profession is so conservative, many of the attorneys she interacted with didn't see the opportunity. After only a few months of blogging, *Crain's Cleveland Business* interviewed Juvan on the use of social media by lawyers. In her first year of practice, she landed a client via social media. That was a game changer, because her colleagues began to see her as an owner, not just an employee.

When she started to land wins, it became harder to navigate her profession because the legal industry was quite competitive. But, as she shares, "I didn't back off, because I now knew how powerful social media was." Good thing. When she was a third- and fourth-year associate, in 2007 to 2008, the economy collapsed. Her class experienced deep layoffs across the industry, which she sidestepped, in part because of her social media efforts. Most of the accolades she has received can be traced to social media. When she was considered for promotion to partner, the fact that she was being followed by prominent professionals on Twitter bolstered her case in a major way, as the CEO saw the potential of these relationships.

According to Catalyst, only 20 percent of partners in law firms are women, and only 16 percent of them have $500,000 worth of business or more.[6] Jayne Juvan made partner at age thirty-two, and at thirty-four, her billing reports placed her in the small percentage of women with $500,000-plus of business. Once Juvan had acquired the basic competencies involved in practicing law, social media became her distinctive strength, propelling her into the partnership ranks at her law firm.

Greg Sorensen, CEO of Siemens Healthcare North America, was able to solve a problem for both Siemens and himself. As a former professor of radiology and health sciences IT at Harvard Medical School, Sorensen is highly credentialed. If Sorensen had raised his hand for a CEO role, however, it is unlikely he would have been a serious contender. But after Siemens Healthcare North America spent a year trying to fill the CEO position with a traditional sales candidate, one of the division CEOs, Tom Miller, and the CEO of the Managing Board, Hermann Requardt, came up with the crazy idea to hire Sorensen: someone who could comfortably converse with CEOs of hospitals and department chairs at major medical schools, speak knowledgeably to the *Wall Street Journal*, and influence the conversation in health-care reform.

Because his unique portfolio of skills met the company's need, Siemens was finally able to fill a critical position, and Sorensen had the opportunity to embark on a new endeavor.

Say Hello to the Low End of the Curve

Now that you've got a handle on your distinctive strengths and have found an unmet need, it's time to disrupt, right? Unfortunately, at the low end of the curve, you're so overwhelmed by new tasks, new people, and new information that finding the *right* unmet need to fit your unique confluence of skills can be very difficult. It's tough to discern between something that is difficult to accomplish and something that is just the wrong fit.

Tereza Nemessanyi (pronounced Nem u SHAWN e) came to Microsoft from a background of strategy consulting and start-ups with the mandate to rethink how the tech giant engages with start-ups in New York City. She dove into the role with guns blazing, ready to shake things up and confident that her past experience and expertise would be taken at face value. What she found was an organizational structure that was difficult to understand and navigate successfully at the low end of her learning curve—she says it was "like I was speaking French and they were speaking Uzbek." She couldn't seem to get anything done.

Finally Nemessanyi's boss assigned her to some projects where she could quickly generate revenue and rack up points internally. She leveraged those projects superbly, and gained the necessary credibility and buy-in to circle back to her original mandate of working with start-ups.

In 2014, Nemessanyi was able to partner with Suzanne Lee, founder and CEO of Biocouture, a cutting-edge biofabrication company and consultancy, to help sponsor Biofabricate, the first-ever conference organized around the concept of growing live biological materials as an input to manufacture. It was hugely successful; the *O'Reilly Radar* blog wrote that it "changed their view of the future."[7] Nemessanyi could have thrown in the towel and left Microsoft when she felt stalled at the low end of her new learning curve, but because she worked through the initial phase of learning and achieving pay-to-play milestones, she was able to build credibility, gaining access to the resources she needed to fulfill Microsoft's unmet needs.

Sometimes moving up the curve just takes patience. In 2004, Lauren Zalaznick had arrived at the cable network Bravo as a result of the NBC acquisition of Universal. The network was looking for a show that would appeal to "affluencers"—well-educated, influential, and affluent viewers. *Project Runway*, a show about aspiring fashion designers, was that show. Bravo chose the airdate carefully. December 1 at 10 p.m. It had a strong lead-in and would air the week after Thanksgiving, when main networks were airing reruns. The network promoted the show heavily. It did everything right. But the ratings were bad. Only two out of a thousand people were watching, when the projection was twenty. The ratings were so bad, the team thought Nielsen had made a mistake. Both the show and Zalaznick's job were on the line. Second-week ratings weren't any better. The third week, ratings were actually *lower*.

So Zalaznick asked, what can we learn? Bravo had never had original programming in the 10 p.m. time slot, so maybe viewers weren't used to looking for content there. Maybe the massive ad campaign of a few million dollars was paltry compared with those of the major networks. Maybe competitive reality shows weren't a thing, and neither was fashion.

But instead of pulling back, Bravo doubled down. Instead of airing shows that it knew could get ratings, the network kept airing *Project Runway*. The idea of binge watching hadn't yet taken hold, but marathoning on cable had, so Bravo aired the first three episodes as often as possible. By January, the ratings had quadrupled. We know the rest. It was the first competitive reality show on cable to win an Emmy, beating the major networks. It was in the vanguard of reality television, and legitimized creative competition on TV. The show wasn't a bomb; Zalaznick and her team were simply at the low end of the curve.[8]

Sometimes you *are* on the wrong curve. You may see a huge opportunity, or hope to be hired to do a job, but before taking the job or starting that business, make sure that you have the strengths that meet those needs. If there isn't a match, it will be tough to drive toward competence. Best-selling author Augusten Burroughs wanted to be an actor as a child, and was confident he would be "one of the greatest actors of the day, possibly the greatest." When he finally saw himself on videotape, "it was a stunning revelation. My knowledge that I was giving an incredible performance in no way aligned with what I saw. I sucked worse than anything has ever sucked in the history of suckage."[9] Faced with the truth that he was not an actor, he wondered, what now? Burroughs eventually made his way toward writing. Because he writes well, he was able to do the job that he had hoped to do as an actor: connect with people. He then explains, "When I chose writing over acting, I didn't give up on a dream, I gave up on my choice of vehicle used to deliver the dream. Dreams are not like spleens, there's not just one per person." Like Burroughs, you may find that your distinctive strengths do not align with the learning curve you are hoping to scale. In which case, you'll want to jump to a curve that is a better fit.

There is no shortage of jobs-to-be-done and problems to be solved. But there's only one of you. The right problems are those that you somehow feel called to solve, and are capable of solving, because of your expertise and accumulated life experience. As you consider making the leap to a new learning curve, examine the assets you've acquired, and focus on what you can do that others cannot. Then look for a job that no one else is doing. Just as Darwin's finches developed unique beaks to effectively get access to food, when you recognize and apply your distinctive strengths, you'll quickly move up the pecking order of your personal curve of learning.

3

Embrace Constraints

Whom the gods wish to destroy, they give unlimited resources.
—Twyla Tharp

Constraint, limit, restriction, shackle, ceiling, cap, regulation, ration: Americans living in "the land of the free" don't much like these words, believing that anything that infringes on our freedom undermines our inalienable rights to life, liberty, and the pursuit of happiness.

But nothing could be further from the truth when it comes to pursuing a new challenge. Constraints offer structure that can liberate us from the chaos and disorder of entropy.

Not only are constraints theoretically good, as a practical matter, they are unavoidable. Did you know, for example, that many of the iconic scenes in *Jaws* came about because of a malfunctioning mechanical shark? The original screenplay called for numerous scenes depicting the shark approaching its prey, knifing through the water and attacking its victims. The mechanical shark was not up to the task, frustrating Spielberg's original vision for the film. Over budget and behind schedule, Spielberg decided to shoot those scenes from the shark's point of view, trusting that the cinematography, intense music, and viewers' imaginations would evoke the heart-pounding fear he was after. *Jaws* swam its way to critical acclaim and box office success.[1]

I'll confess I have a love–hate relationship with constraints. For years, I touted the importance of bootstrapping a business, without any real experience of pulling up the straps myself. But, as I have progressed in my career, including becoming an entrepreneur, I have become a reluctant believer in the power of working within limits. Constraints aren't fun, but they do work.

Constraints Lead to Faster Feedback

Because changing the status quo tends to be unnerving, most of us want feedback on how we're doing as quickly as possible. The most effective and accurate way to achieve this is by imposing constraints.

This may seem counterintuitive. You might argue that if you are undertaking a new venture, you want complete freedom, which will allow you to explore all the possibilities. You may also be concerned that by limiting yourself you will not be able to get where you want to go. To understand why this is the wrong approach, let's begin by imagining what disrupting yourself would look like if you had no constraints.

First, let's consider the math behind a life with complete freedom. While the possibilities are impressive, the complexity can be debilitating. Examine a simple ten-step process with only two options for each step. Doing the math gives you 2^{10}, or 1,024, possibilities. Given enough time, you could probably figure out which path would yield the best result. Now, take this same ten-step process and increase the number of options so that you have three possibilities for each step. This gives you 3^{10}, or 59,049, possibilities—significantly more daunting. What happens when you have complete freedom or an infinite number of possibilities for each step in the process? You got it. Before you even complete the first step you are faced with an impossible number of possibilities. The sheer enormity of options overwhelms.

The human mind has astounding learning capabilities but constantly seeks out constraints. Including constraints allows you to make a faster, more accurate prediction of the consequences of your actions, letting you determine which course of action will likely give you the best result. Think about skateboarders. Author Daniel Coyle posits they are some of the quickest learners in the world, because they receive incredibly fast and useful feedback—every action, every move has an immediate consequence.[2] It's the same logic that leads coaches in numerous sports, including soccer, swimming, and baseball, to shrink the space their athletes train in to create tighter feedback loops.

Shrinking the space can also be helpful when you are looking for feedback on your products or company. Vala Afshar, chief marketing officer of Extreme Networks, is an interesting case study.[3] Trained as an electrical engineer, Afshar joined Extreme Networks in 1996 as a software developer/quality service engineer, eventually transitioning to run the services business, becoming the chief customer support officer. In this role, Afshar became very active on Salesforce's Chatter, a private social network for business, and by 2011 had built a large internal following. As the chief information officer took note of Afshar's intracompany influence, he signed Afshar up for Twitter and gave him the mandate to interact with networks outside of the company.

As Afshar prototyped his ideas in real time, he gained an external following. A publisher approached him about writing a book; his presentations on Slide-Share gained more than one million views; and he was promoted to chief marketing officer. Vala Afshar has become a thought leader, epitomizing a new breed of chief marketing officer, both highly social and highly technical—and Extreme Networks has unusually high name recognition for a $500 million company. Afshar's ability to shrink the space, getting immediate and actionable feedback, was pivotal in expanding his space into a high-profile public role.

Fast feedback is also useful when it comes to identifying your distinctive strengths. Karen May, VP for people development at Google, invented a method she calls "speedback." It works like this: "partway through a training session she will tell everyone to pair off and sit knee to knee, and give them three minutes to answer one simple question: 'What advice would you give me based on the experience you've had with me here?' Participants say that it's some of the best feedback they've ever gotten."[4] When we are willing to impose constraints—in this particular, instance, time—we have a better chance of identifying what is working and what needs to be changed.

Constraints Help Us Solve for One Variable at a Time

If you are trying to move up the curve, and you are feeling crushed by constraints—not enough time, money, expertise, and buy-in—this may be a signal that you are tilting at windmills. And, like Augusten Burroughs, you may need to find a different dream. But it could also mean you need to slow down and solve for one constraint at a time.

Consider the scientific method. The most definitive scientific experiments are conducted when you change only one variable at a time. An example is the experiments performed by Alfred Hershey and Martha Chase. In the early twentieth century, scientists thought that protein, not DNA, was the genetic material in all organisms. Several experiments had caused scientists to question this assumption but it wasn't until 1952 that Hershey and Chase performed the breakthrough experiment that would prove that DNA rather than protein housed the genetic code in all organisms. In their research, they conducted two side-by-side experiments where they changed only one parameter. In one experiment they tagged the DNA inside the virus with a radioactive molecule, which is essentially a molecular tracking device. In the other they tagged the proteins. They then asked the question, "When the virus propagates (i.e., has babies), do the children inherit the DNA or the protein"? The answer: DNA. This simple discovery has been foundational to all modern genetic research, from understanding genetically related diseases like cancer and cystic fibrosis to DNA sequencing and cloning.

The take-home message is that clear thinking, coupled with the right constraints, can lead to unequivocal answers.

Michelle McKenna-Doyle didn't graduate from college and apply to become the chief information officer of the National Football League. Instead, she began her career with a degree in accounting, sitting for the CPA exam and working as a senior auditor at Coopers & Lybrand. Once she had these basic skills, McKenna-Doyle was ready to try something new.

Because Metropolitan Life, a Coopers & Lybrand client, had worked with her for three years and had proof points of her competence, McKenna-Doyle was able to expand into a controller role, managing Metropolitan Life's real estate portfolio. After four years, and having gotten a clear handle on strategic planning, by keeping her functional role largely intact, she was able to pivot into Disney, a new company and industry.

Over the next decade, as the proof points continued to stack up, she was promoted frequently, eventually becoming a VP in information technology, where she overhauled Disney Destination's sales processes and implemented customer relationship management. Her trifecta of accounting, strategy, and IT expertise fully burnished, McKenna-Doyle was recruited into her first CIO role. But only after three different CIO stints, including at Universal Orlando Resort, did she make a lateral move into her fourth CIO role, at her dream organization, the National Football League. She found her job at the NFL, let it be noted, while picking her fantasy football team.

When we patiently isolate variables, we can more easily solve the equation of personal disruption.

Constraints Help Us Stay Focused

In 2012, approximately 420,000 people were injured in motor vehicle crashes involving a distracted driver. Hence the plethora of laws constraining the types of activities you can be involved in while driving a motor vehicle. The inability to clearly survey the landscape around you without distractions can be a prescription for disaster. What's true for driving is also true for disrupting. Constraints can be the perfect remedy if you are having a difficult time focusing or are unable to clarify how you want to disrupt yourself.

This principle is clearly illustrated by observing how our vision works. The electromagnetic spectrum encompasses all possible frequencies of electromagnetic radiation, informally referred to as light. If we had a detector that captured all electromagnetic wavelengths simultaneously there would be so much information that it would be difficult, if not impossible, to make sense of our surroundings. One form of electromagnetic radiation is visible light; our eyes resolve a small part of the electromagnetic spectrum into the faces of people we love, for example. To detect infrared radiation with longer wavelengths, we need night goggles. To see through solid objects, we need an X-ray machine, which sees only shorter wavelengths. In applying limits to the electromagnetic wavelengths we can observe, we gain clarity.

A corporate instance of using limits to improve focus is Intuit, the company that brought us Quick-Books and TurboTax. The VP of product development was given the mandate to change the lives of India's 1.2 billion people. Given this grand vision, one might expect that Intuit would throw a lot of resources at this project. Instead, the company put together a team of three engineers, sent them to rural India for three weeks, and said, "Figure something out."

One afternoon, during a torrential rainstorm, the engineers took refuge in a bus shelter alongside some local farmers. As the two groups chatted, the Intuit engineers learned that the farmers had limited access to changes in commodity prices, and no way to efficiently determine who the highest bidders were on any given day.

Now that they'd identified a problem, you might think they spent money to solve it. Actually, the engineers began to experiment with a basic and very inexpensive solution—no algorithms, no code—they manually texted price and buyer information to the farmers every day for several weeks. By working with a small team, a minimal budget, and a deadline, the engineers came up with a simple, elegant solution. It was easy to iterate, so they were able to get feedback quickly, figuring out what worked and what didn't, and eventually accumulating the data they needed to get buy-in for the proposed product. Because Intuit was willing to impose constraints, and the engineers were willing to embrace them, they developed a service known as Fasal. It is an easy-to-use, text-message-based platform that uses complex matching algorithms to help the farmers get the best prices. Fasal has more than two million active users in India who enjoy a 20 percent increase in their bottom line.[5]

Imposing Constraints

Of course we all need at least some resources to get going. You can't bootstrap without straps or boots. Scarcity imposes a cognitive tax on our brains,[6] and we have no excess bandwidth to even consider hopping on a new growth curve. Take the case of sugar cane farmers in India who were asked to participate in a series of cognitive tests before and after receiving their harvest income.[7] Their performance was the equivalent of ten IQ points higher after the harvest, when resources were less scarce.

But too many resources can become a snare. According to organizational psychologist Adam Grant, increasing resources enhances our ability to make a go of a business or project,[8] but there's an inflection point at which too much money or time or even buy-in actually diminishes our ability. Grant describes this as an inverted U-curve. On the ride up (or in our model, at the base of the S-curve) when you lack resources, it's about embracing constraints. But, once the pace of growth quickens, a surfeit of resources has the potential to thwart progress. We can counter this by imposing constraints, or making the most of those already imposed on us. Here are several types to consider:

Money

One common constraint is money. And that's a good thing. The lack of money makes business owners impatient for profits, and makes individuals hungry for discernible progress. Real estate entrepreneur Nick Jekogian shares, "When I started my business, money was the biggest constraint. I found ways to turn that into an advantage, and ten phenomenal years ensued. When easy money came into the picture in 2007, because I stopped focusing on innovation, substantial problems with our business model ensued, and we experienced significant losses during the downturn."

In 2007, *Entrepreneur* magazine compiled a list of the five hundred fastest-growing companies in the United States.[9] I was intrigued by the various ways these companies had funded their growth, rather than taking outside cash. Only 28 percent had access to bank loans/lines of credit, 18 percent were funded by private investors, and 3.5 percent received funding from VCs: as many as 72 percent of these successful businesses were pulling themselves up by their bootstraps. I believe these companies were successful not in spite of, but because of, their constraints.

A prototype for bootstrapping is Pluralsight, an online training library for developers and information technology professionals. In 2004, Aaron Skonnard and three software developer colleagues launched Pluralsight on a shoestring budget of $20,000. Growth needed to be funded through cash flow, so they were highly incentivized to get the business model right. By 2007, they had grown the company to $2.5 million in revenue. After they pivoted from classroom to online training in 2008 and demand exploded, Pluralsight finally took in outside money in 2012, raising $27.5 million to fund future growth. In 2014, they generated revenue of $60+ million, and CEO Skonnard was recognized as an Ernst & Young Entrepreneur of the Year.

Knowledge

A lack of experience or knowledge about a particular aspect of a business can be a restriction. But this can also have its advantages. After Athelia Woolley LeSueur's career in international development was derailed by poor health, she started Shabby Apple, an online dress shop. LeSueur, who loved fashion, had almost no knowledge of fashion industry protocol or jargon. Because she wasn't aware of the industry practice of hiring an expensive wholesaler to represent the clothing line to buyers, she simply set up an online shop, saving much needed cash and avoiding unreliable partners. The only manufacturer who agreed to work with her gave her just two choices of fabric, and because each seam, pleat, or button in a dress cost extra money to produce, LeSueur kept her designs simple, making the process easier and faster.

LeSueur was hardworking and smart, but her skirting of industry protocol ended up contributing to the success of Shabby Apple, which generated revenue of nearly $2 million in 2014. When you are trying something for the first time, your approach may very well be innovative and fresh.

Time

Several years ago, I had purchased an ad for my blog on Gabrielle Blair's *Design Mom* blog; Blair is the founder of the blogger bootcamp Altitude Summit. I needed new content for my blog every day, but I didn't have time to write that frequently. I began inviting people to guest blog, and to grapple with the why, what, and how of their dreams on my site. The conversation happening on my blog was enlivened and enriched. The stories shared by these guest bloggers became integral to my first book *Dare, Dream, Do*. My time crunch produced value I couldn't have dreamed of.

Of course, sometimes multiple constraints combine. This is illustrated in the experience of the team of NASA researchers who confirmed on October 9, 2009, that there is water on the moon.[10] Naturally, this was exciting news for planetary scientists. But what I find intriguing is the way they made this discovery. When the leaders of NASA's $491 million Lunar Reconnaissance Orbiter (LRO) discovered they had an extra 1,000 kilos of payload capacity, they requested shoestring proposals for a companion mission. Led by principal investigator Anthony Colaprete, a team from NASA's Ames Research Center proposed the Lunar Crater Observation and Sensing Satellite (known as LCROSS), which entailed slamming a projectile the size of a bus, otherwise destined to become space junk, into the moon. Given their lack of time *and* money, rather than commissioning expensive parts for the car-size spacecraft that would shepherd this projectile and analyze the six-mile-high plume of vapor, the team utilized off-the-shelf non-aerospace technology, including equipment used in carpet recycling and NASCAR heat imaging. Not only was this a scientific success, the team (yes, the government) was able to meet a tight time frame and come in under its $80 million budget.

Invisible Constraints

While some constraints are fairly visible, like not having enough time or money, some are less so— the demons of addiction, insecurity, depression, and illness.

Author Laura Hillenbrand suffers from chronic fatigue syndrome, and has been mostly confined to her home for nearly twenty-five years.[11] In 2001, she published the *New York Times* best seller *Seabiscuit: An American Legend*, the story of a champion thoroughbred, a small horse with an inauspicious start to its racing career that became a symbol of hope during the Great Depression. In 2010, she wrote another bestseller, *Unbroken*, the story of Louis Zamperini, a U.S. Army Air Corps lieutenant during World War II who crashed at sea and, after forty-seven days aboard a life raft, was captured and tortured by the Japanese.[12]

"I'm attracted," Hillenbrand says, "to subjects who overcome tremendous suffering and learn to cope emotionally with it." Zamperini himself summed up the secret to Hillenbrand's successful writing career: "because she's suffered so much in life, she was able to put my feelings into words." Every constraint, whether physical or mental, external or internal, can be a catalyst for moving up our learning curve.

Turn Stumbling Blocks into Stepping-Stones

A constraint you don't think about creatively and strategically is just an inconvenience. In their book *A Beautiful Constraint*, Adam Morgan and Mark Barden, experts on how small brands can challenge big brands, provide a six-step prescription for transforming a constraint into something useful.[13]

1. **Move from victim to neutralizer to transformer.** When faced with a constraint, we initially tend to adopt a victim mind-set, believing a constraint will inhibit our ability to realize an ambition. We either go into denial around the constraint or reduce our ambition to fit the perceived impact of the constraint. As we move to the neutralizing stage, we recognize that the ambition is too important to allow the constraint to inhibit it, and start looking for workaround strategies. In the responsive transformer stage, we recognize that the constraint could be the catalyst for a better solution. We may even impose constraints to stimulate thinking, leading to breakthrough approaches and solutions.

2. **Break path dependence.** If you have locked-in ways of thinking and behaving, examine your biases, personal or organizational, write down the six most important words in your organization or your life, and analyze what you mean by them. If "innovation" is your word, what do you mean—disruptive innovation, sustaining innovation, or something else? Then examine how you usually approach the challenge of a constraint. What is your typical approach? How could it be different?

3. **Ask propelling questions.** A propelling question links a bold ambition to a significant constraint. Think of escape artist Harry Houdini. If you are low on resources, what grand idea or ambition can you hitch your wagon to? If you have significant resources and a clear ambition, what constraint could you impose that would preclude you from thinking about the problem the way you would instinctively? This is what Intuit did in India.

4. **Reframe to "can-if."** Think about how improvisational comedy teams work. In a skit, players never contradict one another; each actor builds on what the previous actor said or did. Instead of saying, "No, but," they immediately proceed to "Yes, and." When you come upon a constraint, instead of thinking, "I can't because," focus instead on how the problem can be solved, beginning every statement with "I can, if...."

5. **Seek new sources of abundance**. If you lack resources, find a way to access them from elsewhere. Rather than focus on the resources you control or are given, think of other resources you can access, including those of stakeholders (who almost always have more to offer than you have drawn on), external partners, resource owners (who have a lot of what you need and may also need what you have), even competitors, and then figure out how you can barter with them to obtain the resources you need.

6. **Activate emotions**. If we cannot connect the need to transform our constraint with an emotional reason why it matters, we won't have the stubborn adaptiveness and creative tenacity when our initial solutions hit setbacks. You'll want the full range: fear, frustration, excitement, and love. Emotions are at their most potent when they contrast. This tension prompts us to make a plan and act on it more than positive thinking alone does. When you activate the right emotions, you can move away from the victim into the transformer mind-set.

Whether we create or impose constraints, having a plan for how to make constraints work for you— asking not "Why did this happen to me?" but "How did this happen to *help* me?—is the difference between bracing yourself for a lesser version of you, and moving at a breakneck speed up your personal learning curve.

Constraints Give Us Something to Push Against

Without certain limitations, we are creating *ex nihilo*, and can easily lose our way. A beautiful example of this is the music for *Ave Maria,* composed by Charles Gounod in 1859. He could have started anywhere, but Gounod chose to begin with the constraint of composing a melody over Johann Sebastian Bach's Prelude No. 1 in C Major composed two centuries earlier.[14] By giving himself something to bump up against, Gounod wrote one of the most beloved and enduring melodies of all time. Twentieth century composer Igor Stravinsky, who also drew inspiration from Bach, said, "The more constraints one imposes, the more one frees one's self."

If you still think it would be preferable to sprout wings and soar to the top, rather than having to slog up the side of an S-curve, consider what happens when human beings actually experience weightlessness. While most of us have, at some point, wished we could fly, people participating in zero-gravity flights often get violently ill. In addition to nausea and vomiting, astronauts who spend extended time in zero gravity may experience headaches, lethargy, and muscle atrophy. Our bodies evolved in an environment where stress and strain are the norm. Weight lifting causes microtrauma that initiates a damage response pathway that secretes growth hormones. Weight lifting, not weightlessness, builds strength.

Constraints keep us grounded, and staying grounded gives us traction. Theologian and academic David L. Bednar recounts the story of a man with a four-wheel drive truck with no load on the back.[15] He'd gone into the mountains and was stuck in the snow, spinning his wheels. Instead of just waiting for help, he got out of the truck and chopped wood. With the addition of a load of firewood, the truck was able to gain traction and drive out of the snow bank.

When you disrupt yourself, you are looking for growth, so if you want to muscle up a curve, you have to push and pull against objects and barriers that would constrain and constrict you. That is how you get stronger.

Pushing against obstacles is how AnnMaria De Mars, for example, got stronger. Having studied programming at Washington University in St. Louis in the late 1970s, she was able to get a position at General Dynamics in the 1980s, when "pregnant, female, Hispanic" was about as far from the stereotype of industrial engineer as one could imagine. She also was the first American to win at the World Judo Championships, winning the 1984 tournament in the under-56 kg class.

Instead of settling into a corporate lifestyle, De Mars left General Dynamics to get a PhD in statistical methods. She then went to teach in North Dakota, where she made connections on the American Indian reservations doing consulting, research, and grant writing. While in North Dakota, her husband was in a sledding accident. After several years of complications, he died, leaving her with three small children and many large medical bills. She is now a professor of statistics at Pepperdine, and cofounder of 7 Generation Games, which emphasizes math skills for Native American students. De Mars's ability to use resistance to build strength is allowing her to contribute in a meaningful way.

What I try to remember about resistance is that it is relative. What was resistance for De Mars may be a trifle for you, or it may be incomprehensibly difficult. But whether you are AnnMaria De Mars, Nick Jekogian, Intuit's farmers, or NASA's investigators, you are going to have constraints.

Here's what's important: when resources are at a minimum, successful people dig deep to discover an embarrassment of riches right under their feet and a plumb line to distinctive strengths. They are also more likely to play where others aren't playing—because other doors are closed—consequently taking on the less risky market risk. Constraints invite all of us to make choices and to own those choices, a critical developmental milestone without which we cannot scale and jump to new curves.

In 1954, an editor at Houghton Mifflin read the now famous article "Why Johnny Can't Read," and, concerned, he challenged one of his friends: "Take 225 unique words every six-year-old knows and write me a story first-graders can't put down."[16] It took a year and a half, and at one point the friend was so discouraged he almost gave up entirely.

But when Theodore Geisel published *The Cat in the Hat* in 1957, it was an instant hit. Years of reciting rhymes and creating cartoons prepared Geisel to reinvent children's literature when presented with a 225-word constraint.

For disruptors like you and me and Dr. Seuss, constraints aren't a check on our freedom. As we learn to embrace them, they become valuable tools of creation.

4

Battle Entitlement, the Innovation Killer

You will achieve the greatest results in business and career if you drop the word "achievement" from your vocabulary and replace it with "contribution."
—Peter Drucker

Entitlement, the belief that something is owed to you by life, comes in many guises, and it is on the rise.[1] It is likely to be a psychological crutch, at least to a small degree, in all of us. Believe me, I see it in myself all the time, even though I recognize that my sense of entitlement can and does slow movement along the curve toward the competent, capable person I yearn to be. As we move into the growth phase of our learning curve and gain more confidence, entitlement is a risk we all face. This chapter explores how different types of entitlement—cultural, emotional, intellectual—stifle innovation at all levels, organizationally and individually, and how to resist its siren song.

Cultural Entitlement

A sense of belonging is an emotional imperative. Much of our self-definition relies on building relationships and on institutions that reaffirm our values. But if that sense of belonging becomes so cliquish that we refuse to look beyond our borders and think poorly of other cultures or ideas, then instead of an upward climb, we're on a downward slide. Being culturally entitled prevents us from looking at the world outside our culture.[2] In seeing the world through this single lens, we believe we've got it all figured out. Acting without thinking is easy. Just do what we've always done.

This myopia extends to companies and industries, from automobiles to education to investing to retailing. In one of my early readings of Christensen's *The Innovator's Dilemma*, there was a section that jumped off the page: "It is striking that Sears received accolades such as *extraordinary powerhouse of a company* at exactly the same time that *it was blind to the basic changes taking place in the marketplace*, including the rise of discount retailing and home centers."[3] Because revenue was growing and margins were expanding, and the company likely believed the adulatory press clippings, Sears was blissfully, even willfully, ignorant of the disruption afoot and competitors nipping at its heels.

As we begin to see the fruits of taking the right risks, playing to our strengths, and embracing our constraints, we can start believing *this is the way it should and will always be.* It's easy to become dulled to danger when everything is working.

Antidote: Transplant Yourself to New Cultures

When my husband and I were in New York, he was doing postgraduate work at Memorial Sloan Kettering in molecular biology. In order to conduct his research, he would grow cells in beautiful pink-colored media. But the cell culture never stayed pink for long. In three or four days that beautiful media would change to a dingy light brown. As the cells used nutrients, they produced by-products, some of which are toxic or inhibitory to growth. When the color changed, it was time to wash and replate the cells, putting them in a new petri dish at a lower cell density. We may be very fond of our current cultural petri dish, but if we want to avoid stagnation, we'll occasionally need to change our environment.

A practical and low-cost means of changing your environment is opening up your network.[4] The more closed your network, the more you hear the same ideas over and again, reaffirming what you already believe, while the more open your network, the more exposed you are to new ideas. It can be painful to be part of an open network because you may feel like an outsider, surrounded by people who don't understand how you think. It also requires you to assimilate and manage conflicting viewpoints. But if you resist your tendency to stick with like-minded people, you will have a more accurate view of the world.

You'll also be more likely to have breakthrough ideas. Brian Uzzi and Benjamin F. Jones, professors at the Kellogg School of Management, reviewed ten years of academic research—17.9 million research articles—published from 1990 to 2000 across a span of disciplines and institutions, categorizing the papers as high or low impact based on the number of citations in other works.[5] It turns out that the highest-impact papers were those that included a mix of highly conventional knowledge and novelty, novelty being defined as the references cited in the bibliography that go beyond the usual suspects. If a paper had a combination of highly conventional sources (85 to 95 percent) with a small subset of highly novel ones (5 to 15 percent), the paper was twice as likely to be a high-impact or groundbreaking paper.

A higher-cost but extremely effective way of keeping cultural entitlement at bay is immersion in other cultures. Shortly after my twenty-first birthday, I went on hiatus from university and lived in Uruguay for a year as a missionary. I came to have a genuine fondness for the people, country, and culture, so much so that when I graduated from college, I wanted my career to involve Latin America; I have now traveled to Latin America nearly one hundred times.

Janssen, the pharmaceuticals arm of Johnson & Johnson, offers a corporate example of overcoming cultural entitlement with its launch of an initiative aptly called Immersion.[6] The idea started with two Janssen employees, Annick Daems and Enrique Esteban, who were spearheading an initiative to increase the company's diversity of thought and experience. As part of this effort, they discovered that the majority of employees who were advising Janssen on emerging markets had never set foot in those countries.

They approached Adrian Thomas, head of Global Market Access and Global Public Health, about providing employees with in-country experiences. Under Thomas's leadership, Immersion has become a global health program with a simple mandate: identify specific problems in specific locations, like hepatitis C in Romania or aging in Poland. Then assemble small, cross-silo teams and get them in-country to find ways to better deliver health-care access in that emerging market.

When you are first trying something, you will likely want and need to surround yourself with trusted colleagues and confidants. Creating something new, especially when you are dealing with huge uncertainties, tight deadlines, and financial constraints, is emotionally exhausting—thus the necessity of having people on board who feel familiar and safe. But once you start to get a grip on the future, impose the constraint of seeking new cultures. Just as novelty is important in academic research, new cultural settings are valuable to innovation; the immigrant population in the United States is a terrific example of how the combination of embracing constraints and being surrounded by a new culture can lead to an explosion of creativity. Immigrants are more than twice as likely to start a business as native-born Americans, and 52 percent of Silicon Valley start-ups include an immigrant. Forty percent of the Fortune 500 companies were founded by first-generation immigrants or their children.[7]

Peter Thiel, cofounder of PayPal, makes this powerful statement about the importance of avoiding cultural entitlement: "Doing what we already know how to do takes the world from 1 to n. But, when we create something new, we go from 0 to 1. Unless companies invest in the difficult task of creating new things, they will fail in the future no matter how big their profits are." If you want to keep innovation alive, look for ways to combine something old with something new.

Emotional Entitlement

Not too long ago, my doctor informed me that I was prediabetic. The mature response would have been: "Well, then I will stop eating so much processed and refined sugar." I'm not very mature, so I threw a tantrum. "Sugar is literally my only vice! I *deserve* a cookie." My doctor's response: "Surely you can find something that will make you happy besides sugar."

Ouch. My story is the perfect example of emotional entitlement, the sense that our feelings must be protected at all costs.

It's easy to think our feelings take priority at home and at work. Perhaps one of your colleagues gets a well-deserved opportunity. And you are genuinely happy for her. But a piece of you snivels, "How come I didn't get that opportunity? Why do I even bother trying?" I know I've felt this way. Failure to acknowledge and see the abundance in another person's success is a form of entitlement.

Or, maybe you are a boss or a director of a board and you don't want to hold your people accountable because you'd rather be liked. That's its own guise of entitlement without obligation. But in failing to hold our charges accountable, allowing employees to experience consequences, we slip the noose of entitlement around their necks and, ultimately, ours.

A shorthand means of gauging emotional entitlement is to observe how we feel about money. If we have lots of money, we think we did something to deserve it. If we don't, then life isn't fair. A few years ago, I wrote a blog post blithely sharing how much money I had made one year. I had worked hard, but in retrospect, there was something in my tone that smacked of entitlement. I got pounded in the comments, and deservedly so. Entitlement poses more of a pitfall for people who have been financially successful in the past. A higher net worth leads to the assumption, "I have it, therefore I deserve it."[8]

In a bit of cosmic payback, I have also been the person hurt by someone else's entitlement. In one of the start-ups I backed as an investor, we had budgeted $90,000 for a particular expenditure. At the last moment, one of the senior decision makers unilaterally made changes, none of which was critical, just to throw her weight around. This decision led to a crippling overage of $30,000, a factor in the company's demise. Because of this person's entitlement, the business, jobs, a company, and money (a lot) were lost.[9]

The stock market provides an interesting examination of emotional entitlement. On November 10, 2010, Cisco's stock price dropped 16 percent, erasing roughly $20 billion of market value in a matter of hours. Had something catastrophic happened? No. In fact, this stock market bellwether had just beat earnings estimates by 6 percent. The company reported earnings of $0.43 per share for the quarter, just barely clearing the market expectation of $0.40. Those who follow the market are familiar with the earnings game: deliver an unexpected stellar quarter, and a stock can gain hundreds of millions, if not billions, of market value. But match, or barely beat expectations, and the market yawns, or worse, dumps the stock, as it did with Cisco. Investors had gotten used to the assumption that the stock would outperform.

This doesn't mean emotional needs shouldn't be met, lest we experience the emotional tax, but when we believe we are owed something by life, deserving more than the person to our right or left, we get caught in a vortex of narcissism that makes personal disruption impossible.

Antidote: Be Grateful

To rid yourself of selfishness and entitlement, try keeping a gratitude journal, a list of three things you are thankful for each day and why.[10] In addition to noting what you are grateful for, make it a point to say "thank you" to those around you. Because expressing gratitude requires self-reflection—the ability to admit that you depend on others and the humility to recognize your limitations—it is an explicit acknowledgement that the world isn't all about you.[11]

Each of us has at least one dream that has been deferred, derailed, or died. Eric Hoffer, a Depression-era migratory worker, wrote, "The hardest arithmetic to master is that which enables us to count our blessings." It is sometimes terribly difficult to be grateful in bad circumstances, but the alternative is bitterness.

Perhaps you've heard the story of a group of teenagers on an excursion in the desert: a rattlesnake bites one of the kids. Instead of immediately extracting the venom, the friends go in search of the rattlesnake. They kill it. But when their focus turns back toward their friend, the venom has spread throughout her bloodstream, and her leg must be amputated.

When we are bitter about unfulfilled dreams, harboring a grudge about not getting the life we wanted or even deserved, aren't we letting venom move through our system? Being grateful for the dreams that have (and have not) come true is an antidote to emotional entitlement. When dreams don't work, we can be mad, or sad, or both, for a time, but then we must choose. Said the beloved author Charles Dickens in *A Christmas Carol*, "Reflect upon your present blessings—of which every man has many—not on your past misfortunes, of which all men have some."

Intellectual Entitlement

Another kind of entitlement, more difficult to detect, is intellectual entitlement, a resistance to ideas from sources we deem beneath us. The "other" in this case isn't necessarily less educated; a person who is street smart might dismiss book smarts (or vice versa), the CFO might ignore the union worker (or vice versa), or digital natives could refuse to listen to their analog counterparts.

Or it may be that you just won't listen because you don't want to hear what "they" have to say. Take Brooksley Born, former chair of the Commodity Futures Trading Commission (CFTC), who waged an unsuccessful campaign to regulate the multitrillion-dollar derivatives market. Soon after the Clinton administration asked her to take the reins of the CFTC, a regulatory backwater, she became aware of the over-the-counter (OTC) derivatives market, a rapidly expanding and opaque market, which she attempted to regulate.

According to a PBS *Frontline* special: "Her attempts to regulate derivatives ran into fierce resistance from then-Fed Chairman Alan Greenspan, then-Treasury Secretary Robert Rubin, and then-Deputy Treasury Secretary Larry Summers, who prevailed upon Congress to stop Born and limit future regulation." Put more directly by *New York Times* reporter Timothy O'Brien, "they…shut her up and shut her down." Mind you, Born was no dummy. She was the first female president of the *Stanford Law Review*, the first woman to finish at the top of the class, and an expert in commodities and futures. But because a trio of people who were literally en-titled decided they knew what was best for the market, they dismissed her call for regulation, a dismissal that triggered the financial collapse of 2008.

To be fair to Greenspan et al., their resistance was not surprising. According to psychologists Hillel Einhorn and Robin Hogarth, "we [as human beings] are prone to search only for confirming evidence, and ignore disconfirming evidence." In the case of Born, it was the '90s, the markets were doing well, and the country was prospering; it's easy to see why the powerful troika rejected her disconfirming views. Throw in the fact that the disconcerting evidence was coming from a "disconfirming" person (i.e., a woman), and they were even more likely to disregard the data. In the aftermath, Arthur Levitt, former chairman of the SEC, said, "If she just would have gotten to know us… maybe it would have gone a different way."[12] Born quotes Michael Greenberg, the director of the CFTC under her, as saying, "They say you weren't a team player, but I never saw them issue you a uniform."

We like ideas and people that fit into our world-view, but there is tremendous value in finding room for those that don't. According to Paul Carlile and Clayton Christensen, "It is only when an anomaly is identified—an outcome for which a theory can't account that an opportunity to improve theory occurs."[13] One of the ways you'll know you are coming up against an anomaly is if you find yourself annoyed, defensive, even dismissive, of a person, or his idea.

Antidote: Practice Hearing Dissenting Voices

Listening to dissenting voices doesn't happen auto-matically. It must be practiced. For instance, how often do you write inexperienced people off as not knowing what they're talking about? Instead, try giv-ing a neophyte the benefit of the doubt. According to management thinker Liz Wiseman, author of *Rookie Smarts*, "inexperienced people, whether recent uni-versity graduates or experienced professionals coming from other organizations or functions, are surpris-ingly strong performers. Because they have significant knowledge gaps, they are alert, move fast, and work smart."[14] Remember Athelia Woolley LeSueur, the founder of Shabby Apple? She didn't know how to sew, nor was she aware of the typical business model for a clothing label; these both worked to her benefit. To move up the curve, you need "highly conventional knowledge," or pay-to-play skills, but to avoid getting pushed off the top of the curve you also need to get your rookie on.

Another tactic is to try reframing dissenting voices as important allies. Literature on innovation tends to frame the relationship between spry innovators and the staid status quo as a David-versus-Goliath battle, but the challenge for organizations and individuals is to acknowledge that David and Goliath must work together rather than fight each another. If you are slinging around words like bureaucratic, rigid, upstarts, too big for their britches, you will stall along the curve of innovation.

In her book *Writing to Change the World*, Mary Pipher asserts that "when we are in trouble with pronouns, we are struggling with us/them issues. Pronoun choices indicate who we stand with and who we stand against, and who we choose to call 'us.'"[15] To gain momentum along the curve, cultivate a "we are them" mentality, believing that David and Goliath, constraints and resources, weaknesses and strengths—or, if you like basketball, the five-foot-six-inch Muggsy Bogues and six-foot-ten-inch Alonzo Mourning—are all on the same team.

Finally, you can practice being that outside voice. One of the best ways to combat intellectual entitlement, or the notion that people should buy in to your ideas simply because they are yours, is to do the work of translating and selling them to your stakeholders. Work to build consensus around your ideas, whether your customer is your manager, your direct reports, your children, or the CEO. No matter how powerful you may be, when you have the humility to do the work of getting others on board, you will be able to repeatedly jump to and successfully mount your own learning curves—and help others do the same.

Scott McNeal is currently the chief information officer in GE's Distributed Power Services. Earlier in his career at GE, McNeal was a production engineer at GE Plastics. His mandate was to build capacity and production through automation. This, however, meant the eventual reduction of hours, and therefore earnings potential, of employees on the manufacturing floor. Because rational data, the data that CFOs like, is a lousy way to get cooperation critical to improvements, McNeal factored employee concerns into the mix, allocating a portion of his budget to addressing their concerns. This approach paid off disproportionately in cooperation. Because McNeal did the hard work of listening and responding to his colleagues, they, in turn, were more favorably disposed toward the needed improvements.

Disrupt Yourself
Before Disrupting Others

In Shakespeare's *Henry V*, there is a nighttime scene in the camp of the English soldiers just before their battle with the French. In disguise, King Henry wanders among the soldiers trying to gauge their morale. Because they don't know who he is, their comments are unguarded. A conversation ensues about who bears the responsibility for what happens to the men in battle, the king or each soldier. One soldier says, "If [the King's] cause be wrong, our obedience to the king wipes the crime of it out of us." Not surprisingly, King Henry, still in disguise responds, "Every subject's duty is the king's, but every subject's soul is his own." This strikes at the heart of what it means to battle entitlement. We can natter all day about being agents of disruption, but to effect real change, we need to be the subject of disruption. Innovation starts as an inside game.

There will always be variables outside our control, but to experience the hypergrowth of personal disruption, we acknowledge that certain rules always apply—the importance of embracing constraints, even imposing them on occasion, and leveraging our distinctive strengths while colonizing the right risks.

Most of us are brimming with the confidence, even competence, to change the world. It is vital that we are also equipped with the humility to understand that changing the world and keeping innovation alive require that we change ourselves. Let's not risk losing a lofty dream because we think we deserve it.

5

Step Down, Back, or Sideways to Grow

You have learnt something. That always feels at first as if you have lost something.
—George Bernard Shaw

Sometimes the only way up is down. Think of the diver who crouches down before springing off the board, or the rower who strokes back to glide ahead. It's Newton's third law, which states that for every action there is an equal and opposite reaction.

Disruption by definition involves moving sideways, back, or down, with all the negative connotations that conjures, in order to move forward. As a business owner, you part with profits to acquire the equipment you need to scale. As a manager, you sacrifice some of your own productivity to teach your employees new skills, making the whole team more effective down the road. As a professional, you may even accept a cut in pay or status to take the job of a lifetime.

In this chapter, we'll explore how companies and individuals can take a step back in order to grow, and how a sideways, backward, or downward move can become a slingshot up your personal learning curve.

The Benefits of a Step Back

When organizations get too big, they often stop exploring smaller, riskier—but possibly more lucrative—markets because the resulting revenues won't have enough impact on their bottom line. There are many examples of this. Yahoo is one: in the nascent days of the web, Yahoo flipped the revenue model on its head when it introduced banner ads and shifted to tracking ad response rather than impressions.[1] In pursuing the ever higher margins and greater profits of banner ads, Yahoo dismissed opportunities like content marketing and mobile. These opportunities, once thought too small, or too much of a hassle to pursue, are now making a direct hit to the engine of Yahoo's business. It is terribly difficult to step back when you are getting better and faster at what you are currently doing.

But the benefits are sizable. When you choose to step back, you can consider what you hope to learn or discover—a sort of business plan for your backward move. And, if you are jumping to a new curve, you can prepare in advance so as to enjoy a softer landing, financially, and quite possibly emotionally.

One interesting example of stepping back in order to grow is BRE Bank in Poland. According to Chris Skinner, banking expert and author of *Digital Bank*, after BRE Bank launched in 1988, it grew rapidly, becoming Poland's third-largest bank. Then, in 2000, with the rise of the Internet, BRE Bank launched mBank, a pure-play online bank.

The real opportunity for disruption came in 2011 when BRE Bank was under siege from new entrant Alior. Says Skinner, "Fearing its core market would be seriously contested, BRE Bank invested $35 million over 15 months to reinvent the bank for the mobile, social, digital age and offer services like money transfers via text. It even tossed the BRE name, rebranding the entire group to mBank."[2] In addition to winning 11 global industry awards for innovation, mBank is not only trouncing competitor Alior in innovation, it is again #1 in customer acquisition in Poland, far outpacing industry growth.

At the level of personnel, when you allow employees to rotate into new roles, revenue growth and margin expansion will likely decline temporarily. An impaired ability to hit revenue and growth targets could put your personal standing at risk. But in the long term, it's the smart call for you and your firm. According to an in-depth study conducted by Accenture, high-performing companies, those that surpass their peers on financial metrics across business cycles and leadership eras, are those that develop capabilities *before* they need them.[3] The average and low-performing companies don't.

It is almost always better to step back than to be pushed back, but for nearly every company and individual, pushback at some point seems inescapable. A company may run up against a competitor it cannot beat and have to completely rethink its product or service, or you might be fired from a job despite your best efforts. In either instance, what feels like being pushed off a cliff can launch you to a new learning curve with greater opportunities for growth, profit, and success.

Consider Tractor Supply, a chain of stores for home improvement, agriculture, lawn, and garden care. Tractor Supply was founded in 1938 to sell tractor parts to the six million farms in the United States. Growing steadily, the company went public in the 1950s. But by the late 1960s, tractors were more reliable and didn't need as many parts. At the same time, the number of farms had declined to three million. Over the next twelve years, Tractor Supply was acquired twice, and had five different presidents in one decade. After seeing a significant number of store closings and a revenue decline to $100 million, down significantly from the peak, several key executives participated in a leveraged buyout in the early '80s.

The new owners plowed into the data and discovered that, while the number of commercial farmers was decreasing, hobby farming was on the rise. This suggested a strategic pivot away from supplying tractor parts, and toward general farm and ranch supplies. Says former CEO Joe Scarlett, "One of our key goals was to become the pet supply store for people who own horses." Today, Tractor Supply has grown to 1,400 stores, three times more than its next five competitors combined, with revenue north of $5 billion.[4]

Stepping back can be traumatic personally. Elin Cherry, an attorney and compliance officer who has held positions at Bank of America and Societe Generale, was shoved off her curve when she was fired. Her son immediately asked the question, "What did you do wrong?" She'd asked herself the same question over and over again for about a year, and finally came to the conclusion that neither the question nor the answer mattered. "Being fired was painful," she says, "The time has not been a cakewalk; for the better part of the year, I felt down and was in the throes of a midlife crisis. I doubted my abilities, my past successes, and my ability to reenter the workforce in a meaningful way. But with ample time and no other choice, I plowed forward."[5]

As Cherry put one foot in front of the other, she competed in her first triathlon and three 5K runs, and embraced a healthier lifestyle. She joined a compliance consulting firm that she loves. Cherry discovered that life goes on. She discovered that her career is important, but she no longer places work ahead of family and sleep. She's also learned that people are wonderful. Many have been willing to tell their stories and to listen to hers. Knowing that you aren't alone in the experience of being pushed off the curve helps ease some of the psychological trauma of that unexpected loss. We need to know that we're not alone, life will go on, and we will be successful again.

Just as a company's survival depends on revenue growth, an individual's well-being depends on learning and advancement. For far too many, growth comes to a standstill at the top of the curve. Once we achieve a certain level, it seems there's nowhere else to go—so we keep on doing the same thing. Those who want to grow have to jump to a new role, industry, or type of organization.

This doesn't necessarily mean you need to change employers. Dave Blakely earned a master's degree in mechanical engineering from UC Berkeley and started as a staff engineer at design consultancy IDEO two decades ago. Many people in his position would have deepened their core expertise and eventually managed technical staff. Instead, Blakely became a program manager, a job that many of his colleagues considered to be a step down, a place for someone who couldn't handle the rigor and detail of engineering. But the new role allowed him to broaden his skills: he learned how to delegate and build team morale, for example. Those new skills propelled him into the management ranks, and eventually he became the head of technology strategy at IDEO. Blakely didn't foresee he'd have that role when he started his career, but moving sideways let him climb a more rewarding ladder over the course of his twenty-five-year tenure at IDEO.

Then again, your step back may involve changing

your employer. In 2002, Carine Clark was senior director of network products at Novell, responsible for building a global campaign for an $800 million business. At the height of her success there, Clark left to run marketing (at a third of her former salary) for the unknown start-up Altiris, a SaaS-based platform for managing IT assets. This step back became the launch pad for her personal rocket ship. In 2007, Altiris was acquired by Symantec, a security and storage software company with revenue of more than $6 billion; Clark eventually became the chief marketing officer.

But in 2012, after a sabbatical to deal with stage-three ovarian cancer, Clark took what some would consider a step down to become the CEO of Allegiance, a $20 million software company that analyzes customer data in real time. In early 2015, MaritzCX acquired Allegiance. Despite Allegiance being one-tenth the size of MaritzCX in terms of revenue, Clark was immediately tapped by Maritz's chairman to be the president and CEO. Clark's ability to take calculated backward moves has been critical to her career success. Or as she likes to say, "lose something now to win something that is bigger and better." Let's not forget Clay Christensen. Only after being fired from a CEO role did he decide to pursue a doctorate degree—with five young children and at nearly forty years of age.[6] This backward move positioned him to develop a theory that has changed the way we think about business, and Christensen has become one of the world's leading management thinkers.

Is Stepping Back the Right Move?

Just because there can be benefits to a strategic step back doesn't mean it is always the right call. If you're working toward an ambitious and potentially achievable goal, such as managing a division at your company or winning a C-suite job in your industry, there's no need to. But if as an individual you've reached the top rung of the ladder you're climbing, it's time to find a new ladder—for the same reasons companies must seek out new markets.

First, you need to head off the competition. As you continue to improve along the dimensions of performance that the employment market has historically valued, you risk overshooting demands. What you do reliably, if not brilliantly well, can be done just as effectively by many peers—and perhaps more swiftly and affordably by up-and-comers.

Second, consider the greater rewards that disruption might bring. It's true that disruptive innovation in business tends to start out as a low-cost alternative, and of course you don't want to embrace a career strategy that reduces your own price point. But when you disrupt yourself, you vector to a new set of performance metrics. And with personal disruption, compensation is not just financial—psychological and social factors also matter.

Also consider the phase of your career. Early in your career, you are at the low end of the curve. You can take the jobs that no one else wants. There's little to lose in taking a step back. Senior employees are at the upper end of the organizational curve. If things get really bad, they likely have a golden parachute, and there's enough headroom to slingshot forward. The risk/reward math works. It's much more complicated if you are a middle manager. Trying something new could result in a steep slide back down the curve, with internal fiefdoms giving a none-too-collegial shove.

An HR program manager (we'll call him Ben) inside a storied Silicon Valley company leveraged his distinctive strength of coding to write a program that remediated a departmental pain point. The last thing anyone expected from his role was a full-application ecosystem and operational dashboard complete and in production in less than a month at zero additional cost to the team. His colleagues in IT now had to decide if they would "bless" his initiative and solution, or reject it because he had inadvertently done their job quickly and affordably. They opted for the latter: instead of cheering, they booed.

If you are a middle manager, you likely have had a similar experience of being stuck in the middle. In innovation circles, it's been referred to as the "frozen middle," because this is where good ideas get put on ice. If middle managers could freely skate up and down the curve to where they believe the puck will go, there would no doubt be a thaw. As you consider moves sideways, up, or down, simply be aware of this dilemma—and, importantly, consider it when the people who work for you want to make a move.

Finally, remember to analyze how well your skills map to others' unmet needs. Just because you crouch before jumping doesn't mean you'll dive into a lake. It could be a shallow pond. One of my coaching clients is off-the-charts good at sales; he's raised money for presidential campaigns and sold enterprise software. He would like to move into private equity.

Given his experience to date, this move will be more of a long jump than a hop and a skip, but it's doable. He lives in Boston, where there are a plethora of private equity firms, and he's plugged into the right networks. If he were still in Idaho where he grew up, this would be an ill-advised long walk off a short pier. No doubt he will need to work harder in finance than in sales, so the slope of his improvement is steeper, but he's in the right ecosystem. He can logically make the leap from here to there. To avoid a dangerous fall, make sure the curve you want to jump to involves the right risks for you and leverages your distinctiveness.

The whole point of disruption is to move up the y-axis of success, however you define success, over the x-axis of time. When you disrupt yourself, you are making a conscious decision to move down the y-axis, leaving a comfortable perch, possibly with pay and status taking a hit, on the premise that the slope of your next curve will be even steeper, leading to another period of rapid growth up the success curve. Just make sure you're not jumping onto the wrong grid.

Preparing to Step Back

There are instances where we abandon ship, whether in a business or a relationship, out of fear. The going gets tough, and we get gone. In my experience, the far more common challenge is mustering the courage to jump when you are comfortable. When the status quo doesn't seem all that bad, jumping often seems needlessly risky. So, pack a parachute to make your jump a safer one.

Charles Scott had a plum job at Intel Capital's Venture Capital Fund, and had developed Intel's clean technology investment strategy. He also wanted to spend more time with his young children. He didn't quit his job straightaway. He took a two-month sabbatical to test-drive his dream: in the summer of 2009, he and his eight-year-old son cycled the length of mainland Japan, 2,500 miles in sixty-seven days.

Scott is also a good example of embracing constraints. Because he was taking his sabbatical in the midst of the financial crisis, he wanted to insure himself against a job loss. So, he not only persuaded Intel to sponsor his trip, during which he would blog about his adventure using Intel equipment, but the United Nations named him and his son "Climate Heroes" as they raised money for a tree-planting campaign and promoted the UN's efforts to combat climate change.

Once he finished this endurance adventure in Japan, Scott had enough data to be certain he wanted to change careers, even though this would mean riding away from a high-status, financially lucrative gig. So he saved and planned for two years before finally leaving Intel in 2011 to launch Family Adventure Guy, a business in which he takes his children on endurance challenges linked to charitable causes, and then writes and speaks about their experiences and earns sponsorship dollars.

One of the most difficult aspects of jumping to a new curve is setting aside your ego. In her essay, "Shedding My Skin," Rebecca Jackson writes, "Have you ever let go of something that simultaneously protects and strangles you; something that both defines you, but also suffocates your evolution? Just like a snake shedding its skin, you have to lose something critical to grow, leaving you vulnerable and exposed in the process."[7]

When we take a step down to gain momentum for an upward surge, for a time we will know less than those around us. This can deal a blow to the ego. In achievement-oriented cultures, it is very difficult to look dumb even temporarily, asking questions like, "Am I doing this correctly?" especially to lower-status team members. MIT professor emeritus Edgar Schein describes a willingness to acknowledge that "in the here-and-now my status is inferior to yours because you know something or can do something that I need in order to accomplish a task or goal" as the art of humble inquiry. For many, this can feel very painful. In fact, in some cultures, says Schein, "task failure is preferable to humiliation and loss of face."[8]

Rethink Your Metrics

"A disruptive innovation must measure different attributes of performance than those in your current value networks," writes Christensen. In layman's terms, when you are disrupting you need to find the right metrics to measure *you*, and quite possibly these will be new metrics.

Think about Billy Beane, the former general manager of the Oakland Athletics. Despite being financially poor, the A's became one of the most successful franchises in Major League Baseball when Beane took the helm. As Michael Lewis chronicles in his bestselling book *Moneyball*, the cash-strapped Beane reframed the game by recasting the way he measured performance.

When the A's acquired relief pitcher Chad Bradford from the White Sox, Bradford's standard pitching metrics were respectable, but his fastball came in at eight-one to eighty-five miles per hour, and he looked funny when he threw—the scouts made fun of him. But because the A's thought about measurement more comprehensively than the other teams, Beane knew Bradford was a steal.

According to Lewis, "Chad Bradford gave up his share of hits per balls in play, but, more than any pitcher in baseball, they were ground ball hits. His minor league ground ball to fly ball ratio was 5:1. The big league average was more like 1.1:1."[9] Ground balls don't get hit over the wall. They make singles, occasionally doubles.

Bradford eventually signed a three-year $10.5 million deal with the Baltimore Orioles.

To get you thinking about how you might more intelligently measure your performance on a personal level, ask yourself: How am I defining success? When you were young, success metrics were handed to you by parents and teachers. They likely included what grades you got, which college you got into, what job you got, or how little trouble you got into. Once you've hit these marks, and you accelerate into a sweet spot of competence and contribution, you begin to play by your own metrics.

Consider some forward-thinking metrics in the workplace. According to Dr. Stacey Petrey, vice president in charge of global compensation and benefits at Mylan Pharmaceuticals, "there are additional categories/metrics by which to measure performance. Here are just three: (1) Talent Developer—tally the number of team members for whom a manager has brokered a move into other areas of the organization; (2) Innovator—did they create an environment that fosters innovation as evidenced by the number of ideas generated by their team; (3) Value Integrator (a manager who analyzes and synthesizes information and turns it into a competitive asset)—count, for example, how many cash management strategies came from their division?"[10] These are all contributions that can be measured. When you are willing to do the hard work of asking what should be measured, you can measure almost anything. Recalibrate personal metrics, too. Disrupting your work life has implications for your personal life. A reader commented on one of my *Harvard Business Review* pieces, "I quit my senior position at a research institution five months ago. I had plans to build a freelance career but then my disruption was disrupted as my wife's disruption started taking hold and her consulting career picked up. I put my plans on idle to take care of our six-year-old twins during summer. Spending so much time with the kids forced me to look at things from a perspective of work–life integration rather than work–life balance. Today I took the children to visit my dad in the small village he lives in. I read under the shade of a walnut tree, with two puppies sleeping by my feet as the kids played with their grandfather. A slow day for sure, but I got enough out of it. To your post about different performance metrics, my five-per-month migraines are completely gone."

As this father illustrates, our personal life also has metrics. It's important to consider the metrics by which you measure your life as a whole, not just the career component.[11]

Is simply showing up perhaps the most important metric of all? A look at some of the research has convinced me that Woody Allen was right, and 80 percent of success really is just showing up. According to Keith Simonton, professor of psychology at UC Davis, the odds of a scientist writing a groundbreaking paper, with success defined by the number of citations in other works, is directly correlated to the number of papers that the scientist has written, not to the IQ of the scientist.[12]

Similarly, Rob Wiltbank, professor of strategic management at Willamette University, tracked the returns of the Angel Oregon Fund and found no material difference in the returns of the winners and the finalists in various pitch competitions over a ten-year period.[13] The runners-up had an equally good chance that their companies would ultimately succeed. It's called the equal odds rule. If you want to write a frequently cited paper, publish a lot. If you want a successful business, get to work. If you want to sharpen your skills as a disruptor, disrupt. A simple metric: show up and keep showing up.

Most people hit a point in their lives where they examine their trajectory and consider a pivot. We typically label this the midlife crisis. In disruptive innovation terminology, it's a rethinking of which performance attributes matter. Famed developmental psychologist Erik Erikson describes this as a period of generativity, during which we have a wealth of knowledge and experience, and are supremely motivated to do not just for ourselves but also for others, as we ask the question *What can I do to make my life really count?* The metrics that we use to define success shift as a consequence. Perhaps earlier in your career the metric was money or fame. Now you want more autonomy, flexibility, and connection. These require different metrics of success. Only you can play moneyball for you. As social media and business strategist

Liz Strauss said, "It's not possible for the world to hold a meeting to decide your value. That decision is all yours."

Every time you hop down to a new curve, you have the opportunity to recalibrate the metrics by which you gauge yourself. Just as a business moves from the messiness of start-up life to codifying process in order to scale, as you start to identify the metrics that measure what matters to you deeply, you'll be able to lock and load, then barrel up the y-axis of success. I don't know how you'll define success. Mine is best described by paraphrasing Samuel Johnson: the ultimate result of all ambition is to be happy at home.

As you look to tip the odds of success in your favor, beware the undertow of the status quo—current stakeholders in your life and career, including family members, may encourage you to just keep doing what you are doing. The metrics you've always used to measure yourself are comfortable, and so are your established habits; performing well on your current path is practically automatic. You can almost convince yourself that staying put is the right thing. But there really is no such thing as "standing still."[14] The "use it or lose it" principle applies to our brain cells just as it does to the muscles in our bodies. Neuroplasticity has a reverse function. Connections recede through lack of activation, while continual stimulation of neural pathways keeps them healthy and active, including—and especially—when you step back, down, or sideways.

6

Give Failure Its Due

Nothing is a waste of time if you use the experience wisely.

—Auguste Rodin

You started a company and it went belly up. You launched a new product and not only did it fail to sell, customers actually hated it. You got fired. What happens when you dare to disrupt yourself and then your progress flatlines—or you're tossed off the curve altogether? What then?

There's the plucky Henry Ford quotation, which, admittedly, I have used: "Failure is only the opportunity more intelligently to begin again." Since Ford was eventually wildly successful, this aphorism does reassure me, but it also jauntily skips over the emotional, psychological, and practical complexity of failure. My failures range from the mundane—not making cheerleader my junior year of high school, for example—to the devastating setbacks of being fired and backing a business that imploded. No matter how many chirpy quotes I may tweet out, when I fail my initial response is despondency, pessimism, and the urge to relocate to another city because I can never show my face in public. Ever. Again. I tend to identify with Margery Eldredge Howell, who said: "There's dignity in suffering, nobility in pain, but failure is a salted wound that burns and burns again."

Why We Detest Failure

Our abhorrence of and shrinking from failure typically start when we are children. Researchers Carol Dweck and Claudia Mueller conducted a study that examined how different kinds of praise would affect fifth graders. The children were given three sets of problems. After the first set, the researchers praised half the students for performance ("You must be really smart!"), and the other half for effort ("You must have worked really hard!"). The second set of problems was so difficult that most of the children didn't even get one correct answer. Then they were given a third set of problems—as easy as the first set—to see how the intervening failure would affect their performance.

Dweck and Mueller discovered that the children praised for their intelligence did roughly 25 percent worse on the final set of problems compared to the first, and were likely to blame their performance on a lack of ability. Consequently, they enjoyed working on the problems less and gave up sooner. Children praised for effort performed roughly 25 percent *better* than on the first set, blamed their difficulty on not trying hard enough, persisted longer, and enjoyed the experience.[1]

If you are reading this book, you were probably a smart kid, and smart kids often create an identity based on their achievements. According to the research of social psychologist Heidi Grant Halvorson, "people with above-average aptitudes often judge their abilities not only more harshly, but fundamentally differently, than others do, especially in Western cultures. Gifted children grow up to be more vulnerable and less confident when they should be the most confident...." Halvorson continues, "the kind of feedback we get from parents and teachers as young children has a major impact on the implicit beliefs we develop about our abilities—including whether we see them as innate and unchangeable, or as capable of developing through effort and practice. This is especially true for women. Because young girls are more likely to sit still and pay attention, they are more likely to be praised for performance. In fact, straight-A girls were the most likely to throw in the towel when confronted with a difficult problem."[2] Whether you are a woman or a man, if you perceive your smartness, cleverness, and success as an innate part of your identity, when you fail, the failure becomes a referendum on you.

There are neurochemical reasons we hate failure, too. Organizational anthropologist Judith E. Glaser explains, "Whenever we are in a tense situation or meeting and feel that we are losing ground, our body makes a chemical choice about how best to protect itself—in this case from the shame and loss of power associated with being wrong. In terms of neurochemistry, our brain is being hijacked." In these high-stress situations, says Glaser, "the hormone and neurotransmitter cortisol floods the brain, executive functions that help us manage the gaps between expectations and reality shut down, and the amygdala, our instinctive brain takes over. When the amygdala, or lizard brain, is in charge, we operate in fight or flight mode, with the default response being to fight or continue arguing for what we believe."[3] Fighting feels better than failing. "When you argue and win," explains Glaser, "Your brain floods with adrenaline and dopamine, which makes you feel good, dominant, even invincible. So the next time you are in a tense situation, you argue again. And become addicted to being right." If you're addicted to being right, you can't exactly partake in the kind of humble inquiry that's an essential part of growth. Rather than fight it or flee it, we must learn to face failure. As Harvard psychologist Tal Ben-Shahar writes, "Fear of failure, resulting from often unrealistic and perfectionist demands [is] one of the key detractors from learning, leading to lack of creativity and procrastination. Learn to fail or fail to learn."[4]

Learning to Fail

When you disrupt, you are walking into the unknown, exposing yourself to the risk of failure. While exploring unfamiliar territory you are almost certainly going to misstep. Some mistakes will be inconsequential, leading to delays or inconveniences. Others will be gigantic, earth-shattering failures that will make you doubt your choices or even doubt yourself. As I have grappled with my own failures, and as I have watched others dealing with setbacks, I have observed several responses that seem to ameliorate failure, transforming it into a stepping-stone to future success.

Recognize That It's Not a Matter of If, but When

A few years ago, I walked into a recording studio for the first time. The building exterior was nondescript. Inside, there were shelves of musical instruments, banks of recording equipment, and a grand piano. I was there to play the piano for my friend Macy Robison's cabaret-style recital "Children Will Listen." We were recording in advance of her performances in a nationwide series of inspirational events called Time Out for Women. I was "pinch-myself" thrilled.

As I entered the studio, I was eager but relaxed. My calm was short-lived. Within minutes of meeting the producer and audio engineer, the perfectionist in my head started tearing down my confidence—I haven't played piano seriously since college. Why didn't they hire a professional pianist? They are going to think I'm lousy. I started to play, and I played badly. The more mistakes I made, the more frazzled I became. I hadn't approached this experience acknowledging that it was not a matter of if I make a mistake, but when.

At lunch, Macy advised me to figuratively wave to my mistakes as I would to a casual acquaintance, not paying them too much mind, and to focus on how quickly I could recover. I relaxed. The mistakes began to decrease, and we ended up with a recording we were happy with.

I learned an important lesson in that recording studio. If you want failure to be anything but emotionally catastrophic, you need to plan to fail. Part of that plan, in addition to a focus on recovery time, is surrounding yourself with stakeholders, like Macy, who are sufficiently invested in you that they'll stick with you even through a professional face-plant.

A good example of this is Riot Games, creator of the massively popular online game *League of Legends*. The gaming community is a tight-knit world, and gamers' loyalties can shift quickly as they lose patience with technical or creative failures in their favorite games. Riot has chosen to address its failures by communicating directly with its users and using humor, often of a self-deprecating variety. According to Chris McArthur, a senior game developer at Riot, "The overall effect ends up giving us a much more human face and making us feel more authentic to our players. Yes, you may get pissed off at the mistakes your friend makes sometimes, but he is still your friend."

By not taking itself too seriously, Riot Games has generated fan empathy and fidelity. This attitude of openness to criticism and dialogue around failure has had an effect on Riot's internal culture as well. "We have no 'yes men' here," says McArthur. "Employees are constantly challenging their managers' decisions, calling out failures, challenging convention, and having those difficult conversations. Failure is something that people see happening and see discussed, so is no longer feared. But instead, it's seen as an opportunity to learn something and improve."

Redefine Success

We live in a world where being anything less than the best is tantamount to failure. Figures from the sports and business arenas seem uniquely adept at coining derogatory quotes about not winning. Second place is the first place loser," said NASCAR driver Dale Earnhardt. Former Major League Baseball executive Gabe Paul opined, "There is no such thing as second place." If this is really what we believe to be true, most of us are 99.9 percent failures and .1 percent winners.

An unusual illustration of this false paradigm comes from a 2009 *New York Times* article called "The No-Stats All-Star" about Shane Battier, formerly of the NBA championship team Miami Heat.

Battier was considered by many inside the NBA as, at best, a replaceable cog in the machine of his team. When you google Battier you get lots of shots of the back of his head, seemingly mucking up the shot as the camera tries to focus on all-stars like Kobe Bryant and Kevin Durant.

Interestingly, nearly every team he played on had the magical ability to win. When he was on the court, his teammates got better, and his opponents got worse. It was said, "Battier seems to help the team in all sorts of subtle, hard-to-measure ways, with a weird combination of obvious weaknesses and nearly invisible strengths. They call him Lego, because when he's on the court, all the pieces fit together."[5] Battier's definitive strength of quietly assisting his team wasn't a power position, so despite his amazing talent he wasn't thought of as an "all-star." If you aren't putting points up on the board, racing up the curve, or leaping from one tall curve to the next, by Western cultural norms, you are second best, a polite euphemism for "loser."

Acknowledge and Share Sadness

When I fail, I am mortified, but I am also heartbroken. I have envisioned a future in which I would achieve a goal, and perhaps be hailed as the conquering hero. And then I didn't. And I wasn't. I've learned it is important to grieve.[6]

It has been said by a number of psychologists who

study recovery from trauma that mourning with-out empathy leads to madness. The person who suf-fers loss must be able to give testimony to someone as a way of working through and learning from this loss. We often think of loss of a marriage or a loved one, but there is also the loss we feel when a profes-sional dream—even a small one—is dashed. Author Sue Monk Kidd said, "There's no pain on earth that doesn't crave a benevolent witness." So don't hide your failures, much as you may want to bury them deep in the earth where they will never be seen. Acknowledge them and share them with someone you trust.

Jettison Shame

If you let a failure become a referendum on you, the millstone of shame will drown you and your dreams. Shame and vulnerability expert Dr. Brené Brown hammers this idea home. In professional sports, the military, or corporate life, "When the ethos is 'kill or be killed', 'control or be controlled', failure is tanta-mount to 'be killed.'"[7] Being perceived as weak elic-its tremendous shame. I've seen this play out in my life. I once bombed a speech: by the time I finished, I was perspiring so much it looked as if I'd just run three miles. The job I was fired from? I wondered if I would ever recover. The business I fronted that went belly up? I felt I should have read the situation bet-ter and made different choices. How could I claim to be a savvy investor? We frequently applaud failure in theory, but the dirty little secret is that it makes all of us feel at least a little ashamed.

Any dishonor we feel when we fail must be deep-sixed, labeled as the detritus that it is. If it isn't, we may never again speak in public, throw ourselves into new job, or invest in another company.

Failure itself doesn't limit dreaming and personal innovation—shame does. Once we pull shame out of the equation, we eliminate the drag and gain the lift we need to accelerate back into daring.

Learn from It

As we are faced with interim failures in our personal innovation process, the narrative we construct is key. It's not just about learning lessons along the way. If we want an end-game success, it's about learning the right kind of lesson. *The Lean Startup* author Eric Ries describes this as validated learning, in which you ask: What valuable truth did you discover about your present and future prospects by failing?[8]

Nate Quigley is an entrepreneur who had an idea for a Facebook-esque social media service, but with a twist—he created FolkStory, a shared family journal. The platform launched, and it wasn't a hit. So the team stepped back, listened to feedback, and came up with JustFamily, a cloud-based family photo library. This also failed to find an audience. Now in a third iteration, JustFamily has become Chatbooks, a service that lets users automatically create photo books from the moments they share in social networks and through text conversations. Quigley says: "We blindly charged in with the certainty of being right, and then failed. We regrouped, and listened a lot more carefully the second time. But we failed again. We had to restart once more, this time 100 percent focused on talking to target users about what they very specifically wanted. We made prototypes, showed them to our target users, and iterated based on their reactions until we had a better prototype. It's like we were the 'what not to do' case study of a Lean Start-up, and on our third swing, we followed the Lean instruction manual as carefully as we could, out of necessity, desperation, and related humility."

On a personal note, when I bombed that speech, I discovered when I stood behind a podium it became a barrier that made the speech about me personally, which was nerve wracking. I learned that when I moved away from the podium, I could have a conversation with and connect to my audience. My takeaway from the failed business? Vetting prospective partners is vital, as are clear rules of engagement. "Learning is the essential unit of progress for start-ups,"[9] says Eric Ries. Learning, I would argue, is also a basic unit of progress for dreaming and disrupting. Rather than take failure as a message that you or your ideas are bad or wrong, ask: What have I learned that I didn't know before? How can I apply that knowledge to propel my journey up the learning curve of disruption?

Know When It Is Okay to Quit

One lesson you might learn from failure is that you are on the wrong curve for you. Famed football coach Vince Lombardi said, "Winners never quit." Marketing guru Seth Godin countered with, "Winners quit all the time. They just quit the right stuff at the right time."

Gregory Miller, an associate professor of psychology at the University of British Columbia, and Carsten Wrosch, associate professor of psychology at Concordia University, have conducted a number of studies on quitting, or disengaging from one's goals.[10] They found that people who didn't give up on goals that were not the right goals for them showed increased levels of the inflammatory molecule C-reactive protein. This protein is linked to such health problems as heart disease, diabetes, and early aging in adults. Further, according to Kathleen D. Vohs, a professor of marketing at the University of Minnesota's Carlson School of Management, "if you are pursuing a goal that is constantly frustrating, you will be less successful in goal attainment in other areas of life." In these instances, quitting, or finding a new curve, may be the smart choice. It's important to dream, and it's important to know when to find a new dream.

Advice for the Still Risk Averse

If you're struggling to understand why you aren't taking as much risk as you'd like, consider a technique developed by car manufacturer Toyota called the "five whys."[11] This is a technique that explores the cause-and-effect relationships underlying a particular problem, with the goal of determining the initiating cause of failure. The "five" derives from empirical observation of the number of iterations needed to resolve a problem. While this technique is typically used after product failures to get to the root of a problem, it can also be used to understand why you failed when you took the risk or why you have failed to launch into something new.

For example, a commenter named Ramesh shared, in the comments section of one of my *Harvard Business Review* essays, that after two decades in the IT industry he was bored and wondering what to do next. But he couldn't seem to muster up the will to try something new. Why? Financial security (or the lack thereof) was his initial answer. But then he noted that his net worth was such that he could live without a paycheck for ten years. Still, he was unable to take the risk of switching jobs. He realized that the right question wasn't, "Can I try something new?" but rather, "Why won't I?" Before you can get to the right answer, you have to ask the right question. And then you need to dig deeper and deeper, until you get to the root cause. If you were to apply the five whys to Ramesh's situation, here's what the process would look like:

> *"I have enough money to quit, but I don't."*
> Why #1? "I don't know what I would do next."
> Why #2? "I don't know what I like to do."
> Why #3? "I am always working."
> Why #4? "Working is what I know how to do."
> Why #5? "My job is my identity."

Now we're getting somewhere.

Figuring out a new identity can be one of scariest things you'll do. But once you've jumped off one S-curve cliff, you can jump off another.

If this still sounds uncomfortable, recall the hugely successful people who have suffered through colossal failures. Look at Steve Jobs, iconic founder of Apple, always unveiling the next insanely great product; but he was also the despairing founder curled into a fetal position sobbing on a couch in an unfurnished house when the Apple board fired him in 1985. Or think of J.K. Rowling, billionaire author of the Harry Potter books: just a few years after graduating from university, her marriage failed and she was jobless with a dependent child, diagnosed with clinical depression and contemplating suicide. She would later write, "rock bottom became the solid foundation on which I rebuilt my life."

Dave McClure, Silicon Valley super angel and founder of 500 Startups, also experienced plenty of failure. He skipped two grades in high school and was expected to do great things, but then didn't. He bounced around as a programmer, became an entrepreneur, and barely escaped bankruptcy several times. He applied to Stanford Business School and didn't get in. He worked at PayPal under several different bosses who didn't know what to do with him. But then he started to invest. He realized he was pretty good at picking winners like Mint.com and SlideShare, and he eventually cobbled together 500 Startups with the backing of Silicon Valley's most revered venture capitalists. He is today one of the most prominent super angels in the world.

Whether we see an experience as a failure or a success is ultimately a choice. In late 2014, I was giving a speech to an audience of 2,500 in Portland, Oregon. One of the subthemes of the speech was to persuade the audience to place as much value on feminine characteristics (relationships) as on the masculine (power and achievement), as outlined by Jungian psychology.

Within the first thirty seconds of beginning my speech, I went blank. The technical term is *I went up,* as in, the ideas sailed up and out of my head. Rattled, I stopped and said to the 2,500 people, "I forgot what I was going to say, just a moment." To my surprise, a woman in the audience shouted, "We love you, Whitney. You can do it." With her spontaneous act of kindness, my memory came back, and I felt the most connected I've ever felt to an audience. Rather than a monologue, that speech was a dialogue. This interplay with the audience moved from laughter to sighs to tears—it was an animated conversation.

Later that day, my agent asked me how it went. Based on the power and achievement metrics (how well I stuck to the script, for example) it was my worst speech ever. I had never before forgotten what I had rehearsed and wanted to say. If I measured the speech by metrics that gauge how connected I felt to my audience, it was the best speech I'd ever given.

I had to make a choice.

Did I really believe my own rhetoric about connection rivaling, even trumping, perfection, in certain situations?

Best or worst?

I hesitated. But ultimately, I choose to see the speech in Portland as my best.

I often hear it said that failure is not an option. I agree. Not because failure isn't permissible. It is. Failure is inevitable and sometimes even requisite. Poet John Milton said, "The mind is its own place, and in itself can make a heaven of hell, a hell of heaven." I think this is also true with success and failure. Just as the mind can make of every success a failure, in every failure there can be a success. As you disrupt yourself and sometimes struggle up the steep slope of a new learning curve, remember that failure may be your companion at times. If you welcome failure as a guide and teacher, you're more likely to find your way to success.

7

Be Driven by Discovery

The only way of discovering the limits of the possible is to venture a little way past them into the impossible.
—Arthur C. Clarke

One of the key attributes ascribed to disruptors is that they play where no one else is playing. Whether you are a low-end disruptor or a new-market disruptor, you will find yourself pioneering your way to a market that has yet to be defined. As a trailblazer, even though you may have a goal or purpose, your path to that objective is yet to be marked. It is unrealistic to believe that you can get there without a detour or two; flexibility becomes an important attribute. Hence, disruptors have to be driven by discovery.

Conventional Planning

Picture yourself as an explorer, part of the Lewis and Clark expedition crossing the American West to the Pacific Ocean, starting from the safety of the known and venturing into completely unknown territory. In May of 1804 Lewis and Clark departed from the St. Louis area equipped with keelboats—large, flat freight boats used on rivers—and enough supplies (so they thought) to make the trip. Little did they realize that each new discovery would alter their course and necessitate revisions to their original plan. When the Missouri River petered out, Lewis and Clark abandoned their keelboats. When supplies ran out, they hunted or traded with Native Americans. When they required help, they found a guide and an interpreter. Each obstacle to be navigated drove their decisions for the expedition.

According to researchers Rita Gunther McGrath and Ian MacMillan, discovery-driven planning acknowledges the difference between planning for a new venture and planning for a more conventional line of business.[1] Conventional planning operates on the premise that you can extrapolate future results from a well-understood and predictable platform of past experience. One expects predictions to be accurate because they are based on solid knowledge. In this type of planning, a venture's deviations from the plan are a bad thing.

Most of us prefer the certainty of this kind of

conventional planning. There's likely a checklist with a list of tasks to complete, maybe even a detailed market analysis and a step-by-step blueprint to achieve your goal. If you've gone to high school and college and gotten good grades, you are probably pretty schooled in this type of planning. Do your homework, study for tests, participate in class, and you'll get an A in the course.

A parallel can exist with your career. Beginning in high school, maybe even middle school, you could create a checklist for what you would need to do to become a physician, for example: get good grades in high school, major in a life science in college, go to medical school, complete a residency, and pass your boards, and you'll become a doctor. Once you've checked off each box on your list, you've completed your goal. Under conventional planning, if you don't become a doctor after following this plan, something is amiss.[2]

But this kind of planning isn't how most of us figure out what to do with our lives or even how most companies today figure out how to succeed. *New York Times* columnist David Brooks has said, "Most people don't form a self and then lead a life. They are called by a problem, and the self is constructed gradually by their calling."[3] Matching problems to your strengths isn't just about being rewarded by monetary compensation but also by the joy of following a true vocation. But often, you discover what that calling is one baby step at a time.

Discovery-Driven Planning

With discovery-driven planning, you begin with the premise that little is known and much is assumed. That is not to say that you don't have a plan: you do. It's just a different kind of plan. Instead of declaring, "These are the results that I expect," you ask, "What has to prove true for my plan to work?" According to McGrath and MacMillan, this type of plan includes four steps:

1. **Create a reverse income statement.** If you are launching a new product, rather than forecasting how much revenue you will generate and what your costs will be and then solving for the profit, you build the income statement in reverse. You decide on your required income, and then solve for how much revenue will deliver those profits, and how much cost can be allowed. With personal disruption, the question you ask is: To achieve my baseline level of happiness, what do I need to accomplish and what am I willing to give up in order to make this happen?

2. **Calculate the cost.** With this step, you estimate what the cost will be to produce, sell, and deliver the product or service to a customer. Combined, these are the allowable costs that permit the business model to hold together. As an individual, the question is what kind of time, expertise, money, and buy-in will you need to make your plan operational? Is the personal

cost of being on this curve one you can afford and want to incur?

3. **Compile an assumption checklist.** This checklist allows you to flag and discuss each assumption as the venture unfolds. For example, what assumptions are you making about how much you will sell and at what price? How many sales calls will you need to make to get a single order? How many salespeople will you need to make that many calls, etc?

As an individual, if you decide you want to earn $100,000 a year consulting, and last year you earned $100,000 consulting, then conventional planning works. If you've never consulted, then you'd want to think about the assumptions behind your ability to earn that $100,000. How many clients will you need? How many hours per day will you need to bill, and at what price point? Do you enjoy the work, and will it be emotionally satisfying?

4. **Prepare a milestone chart.** This chart specifies which assumptions need to be tested and what you are going to learn by each milestone. In discovery-driven planning, learning is the essential unit of progress, so a course correction isn't equivalent to failure, as it would be in conventional planning. Rather, it's an opportunity to recalibrate so you can move more effectively up the curve.

A Discovery-Driven Career

At the beginning of your career, it's advisable to take a discovery-driven approach. Let's go back to the doctor example. With this approach, you'll first think about what grades you need to get into medical school, and consider whether you can and want to get those grades while you are in college. To make this plan operational, you'll need high marks in your premed courses such as zoology, biology, and chemistry. After your first two years of medical school you'll decide if you still can and want to make the grade. To test your assumptions around what it's like to be a doctor, you have the opportunity to rotate into various practices during your final two years of medical school. After three years of medical school, you'll have enough information to decide whether to apply for a residency and become a practicing doctor.

If you are driven by discovery, at any of these checkpoints you may decide to alter your course as you evaluate the functional and emotional job that you are hiring medicine to do. Perhaps you love science and want to understand how things work, leading you to a career in research. You may even discover a treatment for a disease or invent a medical device, and become an entrepreneur. Perhaps you'll realize you love systems and efficiency, leading you to a career as a hospital administrator or CEO of a health-care system. Or you get light-headed at the sight of blood but love healing people, leading you to become a psychiatrist.

When you are driven by discovery, you take a step forward, gather feedback, and adapt.

In the real-life experience of jumping to a new curve, new information and constraints interplay with your individual competence. Linda Descano is managing director and global head of content and social media for Citigroup's global consumer franchise. She didn't start there.

After studying geology and geophysics at Texas A&M, she launched her career at an environmental consultancy, where she was responsible for litigation support and expert witness services. She then joined Citibank's (FKA: Salomon) legal division to analyze environmental risk. From there, Descano moved into asset management, where she comanaged a socially responsible investment program, and was eventually recruited to Citigroup's global consumer group to help bring Women & Co., Citi's financial lifestyle publisher, to the marketplace.

Today, she heads social media and content marketing for Citi's consumer franchise. None of this had been her plan. Descano studied rocks in college, but she was so competent and willing to adapt that her managers frequently found new ways to use her, thus propelling her on to new learning curves.

Tom McGuire, a business intelligence analyst at a major retailer, has also tested his assumptions about a satisfying career through the process of discovery-driven planning. McGuire holds both an accounting degree from Marquette and an MBA from the

University of Minnesota. He's spent his entire career within the finance function, and has worked for the past two decades at the same company, but notice the series of experiments he's conducted to find the right fit for him and for the company. Early in his career, McGuire was focused on budgeting and forecasting, and he enjoyed the opportunity to learn a new business, but after a few forecasting cycles, his knowledge peaked and he became bored. His curiosity about other opportunities that would allow him to utilize his skills has propelled him over and over into new learning curves. Ready to make a switch, McGuire would volunteer for a new role. His first management opportunity came in internal audit and accounting. He enjoyed the problem solving needed in internal audit, but the accounting aspect was too repetitive for his taste. He'd begin to tweak processes, agitating for change, which wasn't the best fit for his reports, so he started to look for his next role.

One of McGuire's special projects turned into a twelve-year stint, during which he pitched and created a business intelligence team. As his team's reputation for data, analytics, and reporting has grown, they've been asked to own major parts of systems implementations. McGuire did have an idea of what he wanted to do professionally. He studied accounting and planned to be an accountant, and each position built on that expertise. But his willingness to take a step forward, gain purchase on a curve, then jump to a new curve,

allowed him to end up in a role he couldn't have envis-
aged when he first entered the workforce.

In 2014, Korn Ferry International, the world's largest executive search firm, was trying to understand
what sets top-performing executives apart. Its research
showed that while technical competencies were a
starting point, a leading predictor of C-suite success
is insatiable curiosity and a willingness to learn.[4] This
learning agility includes learning to adjust the metrics
by which you measure your progress. Linda Descano
didn't become a geologist. Tom McGuire isn't a CPA.
Based on the checklist of a conventional plan, both
failed. But they've succeeded by their own updated
measures of success.

You Can't See the Top of the Curve from the Bottom

When you pursue a disruptive course, you'll probably
end up in a place you hadn't anticipated. You won't
be alone. According to the research, 70 percent of all
successful new businesses end up with a strategy different from the one they initially pursued.[5] Millennium Pharmaceuticals, for example, has navigated the
unknown territory of biotechnology and molecular
medicine. Millennium started out as a boutique biotech company targeting treatments for several genetic
diseases. Subsequently, it added genomics, then drug
discovery, then clinical drug evaluation, and after

being public for about ten years was bought out by Takeda as an oncology company. No one could have guessed how Millennium Pharmaceuticals would evolve over those years. Ironically, Groupon began as an activism platform, bringing people together to raise money for a cause or to boycott a retailer, while Netflix, the Emmy Award–winning content company, started as a door-to-door DVD rental service.

When I left Wall Street in 2005, I thought I was going to publish a children's book and produce a reality TV show about soccer in Latin America. Neither happened, but these experiences prepped me to explore a number of business ideas, including backing a magazine that was initially quite successful, reaching circulation of 100,000. The magazine did ultimately fail, a high-priced tutorial in start-up investing. Meanwhile, volunteer work led to my connection with Clay Christensen and founding the investment firm, Rose Park Advisors. When clambering up a new learning curve, you simply cannot know what is going to come next.

This has been the case with Alissa Johnson, former deputy CIO at the White House. After earning an undergraduate degree in math, she had the opportunity to pursue a degree in Management Information Systems, paid for by her government job at the National Security Agency (NSA). The timing was terrible—she started the program only a few days after giving birth to her second child, and her first-born was only 18 months old at the time. Her family, and even her doctor, thought she was crazy to attempt this, but she knew it was something she wanted to do and she didn't let the obvious constraints of her situation stop her.

Being highly driven, Johnson shares that after learning a high school classmate had gotten their PhD, within a month she was enrolled to receive hers. Over her career, she has worked for various Intelligence Agencies and Department of Defense organizations, where she was respected and well-remunerated.

When President Obama was elected in 2008, she applied on-line for a job in his administration, and was eventually offered the job of Deputy CIO at the White House. Though the job required a huge pay cut and a lot of sacrifice, Johnson says of her move, "I was determined to be an asset to the organization. I knew that if I did well then I would be rewarded. Sometimes you have to take a few steps laterally, or even backward to make a difference in your future." Today Dr. Johnson is the Chief Information Security Officer at Stryker Corporation.

Follow Your North Star

One of the things that the textbooks on disruption shy away from mentioning is that discovery-driven learning is often lonely and sometimes scary. Businesses and individuals that are disrupting themselves frequently find themselves with very little, if any, company. After the initial rush of excitement wore off when I left Wall

Street, I occasionally felt a total loss of identity. I could no longer call people and say, "This is Whitney Johnson from Merrill Lynch." Now, it was just "This is Whitney Johnson...." And there have been more than a few days when the p/e, or puke/excitement, ratio has been so uncomfortably high, I feel like I am on a thrill ride to zero cash flow. The path of discovery is rarely strewn with rose petals, but the outcome is worth the struggle.

Because she couldn't see the end from the beginning, Susan Cain struggled through years of insecurity about the kernel of an idea that became *Quiet*, one of the best-selling books of 2012.

Cain wanted to write about how modern Western culture misunderstands and undervalues the traits and capabilities of introverted people, leading to a waste of talent and a loss of self-esteem for the "quiet" individuals among us. Prior to writing *Quiet*, Cain was making a living teaching negotiation tactics to women. Her friends and colleagues questioned the topic she wanted to write about because it wasn't something she had a specialty in, and the literary agents she queried thought it wasn't commercial enough to sell books.

But Cain believed she had something important to share. Her father is an introverted doctor and it was clear to her that his strength as a physician is his temperament. Every day he would come home from work, have dinner, and pore over medical journals. It was the same with her grandfather, who was a rabbi. He was always reading, always thinking, and that's what made his sermons and rabbinical thought so rich.

Cain first had the idea for *Quiet* in 2005. She spent a year writing a proposal. After she found Richard Pine, an agent who thought her idea was marketable, she was swept up in meeting with twelve different publishers; nine of them bid on the book. "This was the most exciting thing that had ever happened to me," she shares.

Then came the long and tortured process of actually writing the book. She was confident she wanted to be a writer, but she had never written a book. In 2007, "I turned in an extremely crappy first draft. My editor took one look at it and said, 'Start over, from scratch. Take all the time you need.' I was relieved and grateful."

Four years later, she turned in the final draft of her manuscript; the book was published in 2012. Cain has written a *New York Times* bestseller, become the leader of a movement for the quiet half of the population, and is now CEO of the Quiet Revolution, because she was willing to persevere in the lonely pursuit of her disruptive idea.

If it's scary and lonely, does it mean you shouldn't disrupt? It may just mean you are on the right track. In fact, if you don't disrupt when you feel you are called to do so, you'll die inside just a little. There's even a name for it: the innovator's dilemma. Whether you innovate or not, you risk downward mobility.

Because disruption can feel like you are in the company of one, you need to know what job you want this learning curve to do. What do you hope to gain and why are you disrupting yourself or your business? You may be thinking, I don't know what my "why" is. Finding your why is part of the discovery-driven process, and there are often clues to be found in your hopes and dreams. Almost any dream can germinate into a reason for disruption, whether it's being your own boss, doing something you love, financial gain, or all of the above.

Lisa McLeod stumbled upon this lesson. She had just finished a six-month-long double-blind study of the sales force of a major biotech firm, in order to determine which behaviors separated top performers from average ones. Her study revealed something that no one expected: the top performers had a far more pronounced sense of purpose than their average-performing counterparts. This was vividly illustrated in a curbside conversation with a sales rep at the Phoenix, Arizona, airport. She was finishing a two-day ride along with this rep as part of her deep dive into the firm's sales process and asked: "What do you think about when you go on sales calls?"

The sales rep shared that she always thinks about a particular patient who came up to her one day during a call on a doctor's office. She recounts, "I was standing in the hallway talking to one of the doctors [wearing my company name tag]...when an elderly woman taps me on the shoulder. 'Excuse me, miss, are you

from the company that makes drug X?' 'Yes, ma'am.'
'I just want to thank you,' she said. 'Before my doctor
prescribed your drug, I barely had enough energy to
leave the house. But now I can visit my grandkids. I
can get down on the floor and play with them. I can
travel. So thank you. You gave me back my life.' "

The sales rep continued, "I think about that woman
every day. If it's 4:30 on a rainy Friday afternoon,
other sales reps go home. I don't. I make the extra
sales call because I know I'm not just pitching a product. I'm saving people's lives. That grandmother is my
higher purpose."[6]

Once you know your why, there are lots of roads
that will take you there. Consider, for example, the
journey of a solitary e-mail message. Whenever you
send an e-mail, it is broken up into packets. Those
packets may travel the same route as all of the other
packets in the message, or none of the routes. Ultimately, the route the packet travels is irrelevant, as
long as the e-mail gets to the recipient. Someone like
Elon Musk doesn't care how many different, unusual
paths he has to take to get where he's going. His driving passion is environmentally friendly technologies—
but he's expressed it in many different ways over the
past decade, from solar power to electric cars to space
travel.

A generation earlier, Kay Koplovitz was capti-
vated by science fiction author and futurist Arthur C.
Clarke's passion for geosynchronous-orbiting satel-
lites. While a student at the University of Wisconsin

in the late '60s, Koplovitz wrote her master's thesis on the impact that satellite-delivered programming could have on governments, cultures, and human rights around the world.

In the mid-'70s, she got the chance to build the cable television business she had dreamed of for UA-Columbia. She became the first woman president of a television network, founding USA Network and the Sci-Fi Channel. In 1996, the business she had built from scratch was sold for $4.5 billion.

Here's the genesis of her why. When USA Networks was sold for $.5bn, she didn't get a cent. From that experience her reason for disruption was born.

In 2000, Koplovitz cofounded Springboard Enterprises, a nonprofit accelerator to help women founders gain access to capital. Her cable business model was highly disruptive, but with less than 2 percent of all venture funding going to women, Springboard really put her out on the frontier. Fifteen years later, more than five hundred companies have been through the accelerator and 83 percent of those companies have been funded. Because her drive for parity persists, Koplovitz is now launching the Springboard Fund, which will invest in women-led businesses. When we know our why, instead of fearing the unknown, we can experience discovery patiently and with dogged determination.

As you embark on a journey of personal disruption, you are in search of a yet-to-be-defined market. Like Lewis and Clark, you have a plan: to discover and conquer new territory. It will sometimes feel scary and lonely, and you will undoubtedly end up in places you haven't anticipated. But your willingness to do things differently than they've always been done will help you successfully discover your way up the S-curve of personal disruption.

Afterword

*My passion for surfing was greater
than my fear of sharks.*
—Bethany Hamilton

Ralph Waldo Emerson said, "Beauty is the moment of transition, as if the form were just ready to flow into other forms." But when one has just jumped to a new curve, plunging into the abyss of a transition, beauty isn't the first word that comes to mind.

In music, a transition is defined as a moment of modulation, a passing from one key to the next. In physics, it's described as a change which results in the transformation of physical properties such as ice to water to steam. When we write an essay, it's the sentence or passage that connects one topic to the next. More generally, *trans* means "a going across." Whether we are transplanting or transacting, exchanging the old for a reimagined self, the classic S-curve can help us navigate the transition.

The more you disrupt, the better you'll get at it. Like

surfing, it is incredibly hard at first. But with practice, it becomes exhilarating.

On this score, one piece of research I find especially powerful comes from famed mathematician Benoit Mandelbrot.[1] For decades, the "random walk" model of stock prices prevailed. It postulates that stock prices will go up or down with equal probability. Modern portfolio theory was largely built on this premise—that stock prices are statistically independent. Mandelbrot proved that prices are not independent. Financial prices have a "memory" of sorts. This is borne out in my experience of picking stocks—they have a personality. If a price takes a big leap up or down, there is a measurably greater likelihood that the stock will move just as violently the next day. What a company does today—a merger, a spinoff, a critical product launch—shapes what the company will look like a decade hence; in the same way, its stock-price movements today will influence stock-price movements tomorrow. Seems obvious, doesn't it? But it wasn't, until Mandelbrot.

Learning is not linear, but exponential: there is a cumulative and compounding effect. If you do something disruptive today, then the probability that you can be disruptive tomorrow increases. Momentum creates momentum.

Staying with what you already know may seem like the safer thing to do, but as Saul Kaplan, chief catalyst at the Business Innovation Factory, shared with me:

"My life has been about searching for the steep learning curve because that's where I do my best work. When I do my best work, money and stature have always followed."

Like a novice trapeze artist letting go of the old to leap to the new, we are sure to experience a moment of midair terror. But we are far less likely to fall if we fling ourselves onto the next curve. And, in the seemingly terrible moment of transition, your dreams—the engine of disruption—will buoy you. *Are you ready to jump?*

Notes

Introduction

1. C. M. Christensen, R. Alton, C. Rising, and A. Waldeck, "The Big Idea: The New M&A Playbook." from *Harvard Business Review*, March 2011, accessed March 5, 2015, https://hbr.org/2011/03/the-big-idea-the-new-ma-playbook/ar/1.

2. W. Johnson, J.C. Mendez, "Throw Your Life a Curve," *Harvard Business Review*, September 3, 2012, accessed March 5, 2015, https://hbr.org/2012/09/throw-your-life-a-curve/.

Chapter 1

1. A. Pascual-Leone, A. Amedi, F. Fregni, and L. B. Merabet, "The Plastic Human Brain Cortex," *Annual Review of Neuroscience* Volume 28 (2005): 377–401.

2. Duhigg, C., *The Power of Habit* (New York: Random House, 2012). Page 17.

3. A. W. Ulwick, "Turn Customer Input into Innovation." *Harvard Business Review*, March 4, 2002.

4. J. Rangaswami, "Thinking More About Twitter, Chatter and Knowledge Worker Pheromones." *Confused of Calcutta* blog, April 24, 2011, accessed October 30, 2014,

http://confusedofcalcutta.com/2011/04/24/thinking
-more-about-twitter-chatter-and-knowledge-worker
-pheromones/.

5. Mark Burnett, Clay Newbill, and Phil Gurin, executive producers, *Shark Tank,* Season 6, Episode 2, aired on ABC September 26, 2014, accessed October 30, 2014, http://abc.go.com/shows/shark-tank/episode-guide/ season-06/602-season-6-premiere-roominate-wedding -wagon-floating-mug-and-kronos-golf.

6. W. Johnson, "Thank You For Doing Your Job."*Harvard Business Review*, January 11, 2011, accessed October 30, 2014, http://blogs.hbr.org/2011/01/thank-you-for-doing -your-job/.

7. P. F. Rollins, 42 *Rules for Your New Leadership Role* (Super Star Press, 2011). Page 8.

8. W. Johnson, "Thank You For Doing Your Job." *Harvard Business Review*, January 11, 2011, accessed October 30, 2014, http://blogs.hbr.org/2011/01/thank-you-for-doing -your-job/.

9. M. Hsu, M. Bhatt, R. Adolphs, D. Tranel, and C. F. Camerer, "Neural Systems Responding to Degrees of Uncertainty in Human Decision-Making," *Science* Volume 310, Issue 5754 (2005). Pages 1680-1683.

10. W. Johnson, "It's Time to Dream For a Living," *Linkedin*, accessed April 23, 2015, https://www.linkedin.com/ pulse/20130822122525-3414257-it-s-time-to-dream -for-a-living.

11. L. G. Dugatkin, "The Evolution of Risk Taking," Dana Foundation, January 1, 2013, accessed October 30, 2014, http://www.dana.org/cerebrum/default.aspx?id=39485.

12. L. G. Dugatkin, "Female Mating Preference for Bold Males in the Guppy *Poecilia reticulate*," *Proceedings of the National Academy of Science of the United States of America* Volume 93 (1996). Pages 10262-10267.

13. H. G. Halvorson and E. T. Higgins, *Focus* (New York: Hudson Street Press, 2013). Page xi.

14. M. Hsu, M. Bhatt, R. Adolphs, D. Tranel, and C. F. Camerer, "Neural Systems Responding to Degrees of Uncertainty in Human Decision-Making," *Science* Volume 310, Issue 5754 (2005). Pages 1680-1683

15. C. Christensen, *The Innovator's Dilemma* (Cambridge, MA: Harvard Business School Press, 1997). Page 143-146.

16. C. Christensen, R. Alton, C. Rising, and A. Waldeck, "The Big Idea: The New M&A Playbook," *Harvard Business Review*, March 2011, accessed March 5, 2015, https://hbr.org/2011/03/the-big-idea-the-new-ma-play book/ar/1.

17. S. Kaplan, "How Not to get 'Netflixed,'" *Fortune* magazine, accessed October 11, 2011, http://fortune .com/2011/10/11/how-not-to-get-netflixed/

18. M. Grush, "Blazing the Trail: Competency Based Education at SNHU." *Campus Technology,* December 13, 2013, accessed January 5, 2015, http://campustechnology .com/articles/2013/12/18/competency-based-education -at-snhu.aspx.

19. D. Tuttle, "Cortisol." *Life Extension Magazine*, July 2004, accessed October 30, 2014, http://www.lef.org/ magazine/2004/7/report_cortisol/Page-01.

20. Sheldon, K. M., R. M. Ryan, L. J. Rawsthorne, and B. Ilardi, "Trait Self and True Self: Cross-Role Variation in the Big Five Personality Traits with Psychological Authenticity and Subjective Well-Being," *Journal of Personal and Social Psychology* Volume 73, Issue 6 (1997). Pages 1380-1391.

21. M. Iansiti and R. Levien, "Strategy for Small Fish," Harvard Business School, August 23 2004, accessed March 19, 2015, http://hbswk.hbs.edu/item/4331.html.

Chapter 2

1. S. Bienkowski, "1-on-1: Marcus Buckingham.", *Success*, November 29 2009, accessed January 5, 2015, http://www.success.com/article/1-on-1-marcus-buckingham.

2. A. M. Isen, "Missing in Action in the AIM: Positive Affects Facilitation of Cognitive Flexibility, Innovation and Problem Solving," *Psychological Inquiry* Volume 13, Issue 1 (2002) Pages 57-65.

3. W. Johnson, "How to Identify Your Disruptive Skills," *Harvard Business Review,* October 4, 2010, accessed January 5, 2015, https://hbr.org/2010/10/how-to-identify-your-disruptiv.

4. Johnson, "How to Identify Your Disruptive Skills."

5. W. Johnson, "Disrupt Yourself," *Harvard Business Review*, September 1, 2014. Pages 130-134.

6. Catalyst. (2014, December 10). Percentage of Women Partners in Law Firms from 1995-2013. Accessed January 5, 2015, from http://prod.catalyst.org/knowledge/percentage-women-partners-law-firms-1995-2013-us-select-years.

7. M. Loukides, "The Revolution in Biology Is Here, Now," *O'Reilly Radar* blog, December 9, 2014, accessed March 15, 2015, http://radar.oreilly.com/2014/12/the-revolution-in-biology-is-here-now.html.

8. https://www.linkedin.com/pulse/20140428103509-302586666-career-curveballs-how-project-runway-flopped.

9. Augusten Burroughs, "Two Minute Memoir: How to Ditch a Dream." (2012, May 1). *Psychology Today,* May 1, 2012, accessed January 5, 2015, from http://www.psychologytoday.com/articles/201206/two-minute-memoir-how-ditch-dream.

Chapter 3

1. R. Lambie, "The Production Nightmare That Made Jaws a Classic." Den of Geek, September 5, 2012, accessed January 5, 2015, http://www.denofgeek.com/movies/22547/the-production-nightmares-that-made-jaws-a-classic.

2. D. Coyle, "How to Get Better Feedback," *The Talent Code* blog, January 7, 2013, accessed January 5, 2015, http://thetalentcode.com/2013/01/07/how-to-get-better-feedback/.

3. E. Carson, "Vala Afshar: CMO, Writer, Twitter, Storyteller, Future Restaurant Owner." *TechRepublic* blog, August 8, 2014, accessed January 5, 2015, http://www.techrepublic.com/article/vala-afshar-cmo-writer-twitter-storyteller-future-restaurant-owner/.

4. A. Bryant, "Conquering Your Fears of Giving Feedback." *New York Times,* December 29, 2012, accessed January 5, 2015, http://www.nytimes.com/2012/12/30/business/karen-may-of-google-on-conquering-fears-of-giving-feedback.html?pagewanted=2.

5. Fasal Intuit, January 5, 2015, accessed January 5, 2015, http://fasal.intuit.com/.

6. L. Starecheski, "This Is Your Stressed-Out Brain on Scarcity," National Public Radio *Shots* blog, July 14, 2014, accessed March 7, 2015, http://www.npr.org/blogs/health/2014/07/14/330434597/this-is-your-stressed-out-brain-on-scarcity.

7. World Bank, *World Development Report 2015 Explores "Mind, Society, and Behavior,"* World Bank, December 2, 2014, accessed March 7, 2015, http://www.worldbank.org/en/news/feature/2014/12/02/world-development-report-2015-explores-mind-society-and-behavior.

8. A. Grant and B. Schwartz "Too Much of a Good Thing." *Perspectives on Psychological Science* Volume 6, Issue 1, (2011). Pages 61-76.

9. *Entrepreneur* magazine, "*Entrepreneur* magazine's Hot 500," July 31, 2007, accessed January 5, 2015, http://www.entrepreneur.com/article/181886.

10. K. Chang, "Water Found on Moon, Researchers Say." *New York Times*, November 13, 2009, accessed January 5, 2015, http://www.nytimes.com/2009/11/14/science/14moon.html?_r=1&.

11. S. Oney, "The Defiant Ones." *Wall Street Journal*, November 12, 2010, accessed January 5, 2015, http://www.wsj.com/articles/SB10001424052748703514904575602540345409292.

12. W. S. Hylton, "The Unbreakable Laura Hillenbrand." *New York Times,* December 18, 2014, accessed January 5, 2015, http://www.nytimes.com/2014/12/21/magazine/the-unbreakable-laura-hillenbrand.html?_r=0.

13. A. Morgan and M. Barden, *A Beautiful Constraint* (Hoboken, NJ: John Wiley & Sons, 2015). Pages 216-219.

14. Thanks to Kristine Haglund for sharing this story and for pointing out that Bach's piece itself arose from a very rigid set of constraints—Bach set out to demonstrate the new(ish) concept of "tempering" musical tones, by going through all "tones and semitones," thus climbing the twelve semitones from C to B and presenting a Prelude and a Fugue for each tone in both a major and a minor key—all kinds of self-imposed constraints. It's exactly that constraint that gives the Romantics who followed (like Gounod and even Stravinsky) something to push against, and makes the "rule-breaking" emotional excess of Romanticism feel so powerful.

15. D. A. Bednar, "Bear Up Their Burdens with Ease," The Church of Jesus Church of Latter-day Saints, April 2014, accessed January 5, 2015, https://www.lds

.org/general-conference/2014/04/bear-up-their
-burdens-with-ease?lang=eng.

16. Sturt, D., *Great Work* (New York: McGraw-Hill, 2014).
    Page 30.

Chapter 4

1. J. Twenge and J. Foster, "Birth Cohort Increases in Narcissistic Personality Traits Among American College Students, 1982-2009," *Social Psychology and Personality Science* Volume 1, Issue 1, (2010). Pages 99-106.

2. M. Heffernan, *Willful Blindness* (New York: Walker Publishing Company, 2010). Page 7.

3. C. Christensen, *The Innovator's Dilemma* (Cambridge, MA: Harvard Business School Press, 1997). Page xii.

4. Michael Simmons, "The No. 1 Predictor of Career Success According to Network Science," *Forbes*, January 14, 2015, accessed March 6, 2015, http://www.forbes.com/sites/michaelsimmons/2015/01/15/this-is-the-1-predictor-of-career-success-according-to-network-science/.

5. B. Uzzi, S. Mukherjee, M. Stringer, and B. Jones, "Atypical Combinations and Scientific Impact," *Science* Volume 342, Issue 6257 (2013). Pages 468-472.

6. W. Johnson, "To Innovate in a Big Company, Don't Think 'Us Against Them,'" *Harvard Business Review,* September 23, 2014, https://hbr.org/2014/09/to-innovate-in-a-big-company-dont-think-us-against-them/.

7. *Economist,* "The Jobs Machine," *Economist,* April 13 2013, http://www.economist.com/news/business/21576101-start-ups-founded-immigrants-are-creating-jobs-all-over-america-jobs-machine.

8. P. Piff, "Wealth and the Inflated Self," *Personality and Social Psychology Bulletin* December 19, 2013. Pages 34-49.

9. D. Rauch et al., "Failure Chronicles," *Harvard Business Review*, April 2011, https://hbr.org/2011/04/failure-chronicles/sb7.

10. J. Tierney, "A Serving of Gratitude May Save the Day," *New York Times*, November 21, 2011, http://www.nytimes.com/2011/11/22/science/a-serving-of-gratitude-brings-healthy-dividends.html?_r=1.

11. M. Beck, "Thank You. No, Thank You," *Wall Street Journal*, November 23, 2010, http://www.wsj.com/articles/SB10001424052748704243904575630541486290052.

12. Mark Kirk, writer, director, producer, "The Warning," *Frontline*, aired on Public Broadcast System, October 20 2009, http://www.pbs.org/wgbh/pages/frontline/warning/.

13. P. R. Carlile and C. M. Christensen, "The Cycle of Theory Building in Management Research," *Harvard Business Review*, July 5, 2006, http://hbswk.hbs.edu/item/5422.html.

14. L. Wiseman, "Why Your Team Needs Rookies," *Harvard Business Review*, October 2, 2014, https://hbr.org/2014/10/why-your-team-needs-rookies.

15. M. Pipher, *Writing to Change the World* (New York: Riverhead Books, 2006). Page 139.

Chapter 5

1. W. Johnson, "Digging Deeper, Yahoo Is Still Being Disrupted," LinkedIn, February 7, 2014, https://www.linkedin.com/pulse/20140207144449-3414257-digging-deeper-yahoo-the-disrupter-is-being-disrupted.

2. Chris Skinner, "mBank: The World's First Mobile Social Bank within a Bank, *Financial Services Club Blog*, The Finanser. (June 19, 2013). Retrieved from The Finanser: http://thefinanser.co.uk/fsclub/2013/06/

mbank-the-worlds-first-mobile-social-bank-within-a-bank.html.

3. P. Nunes and T. Breene, *Jumping the S-Curve* (Boston: Harvard Business Review Press, 2011). Pages 152–156.

4. Joe Scarlett, Keynote at TN Governor's Conference for Economic Development. Joe Scarlett.com, accessed March 19, 2015, http://joescarlett.com/videos.html.

5. E. Cherry, "The Unexpected and Wonderful Lessons of Being Fired," *Forbes*, January 22, 2015, http://www.forbes.com/sites/ellevate/2015/01/22/the-unexpected-and-wonderful-lessons-of-being-fired/.

6. C. M. Christensen, J. Allworth, and K. Dillon, *How Will You Measure Your Life?* (New York: Harper Collins, 2012). Page 51.

7. W. Johnson, "Rebecca Jackson: Under the Skin," *Whitney Johnson* blog, September 11 2012, http://whitneyjohnson.com/rebecca-jackson-under-the-skin/.

8. E. H. Schein, *Humble Inquiry* (San Francisco: Berrett-Koehler Publishers, 2013). Page 18.

9. Lewis, M., *Moneyball* (New York: W.W. Norton & Company, 2011). Page 242.

10. Johnson, W., "Your Own Kind of Moneyball." *Harvard Business Review*, November 8, 2010, https://hbr.org/2010/11/your-own-kind-of-moneyball-the/.

11. Christensen, C. M., Allworth, J., & Dillon, K. (2012). *How Will You Measure Your Life?* New York: Harper Collins.

12. F. Johansson, *The Click Moment* (New York: Penguin, 2012). Pages 149-150.

13. R. Wiltbank, "Robert Wiltbank," Willamette University, March 19, 2015, http://www.willamette.edu/~wiltbank/seattle_angel_conference_may_2012.html.

14. Sylvia Vorhauser-Smith, *The Neuroscience of Learning and Development*, Page Up People, March 19, 2015, http://

www.pageuppeople.com/wp-content/uploads/2012/
06/Neuroscience-of-Learning-and-Development1.pdf.

Chapter 6

1. C. M. Mueller and C. S. Dweck, "Praise for Intelligence Can Undermine Children's Motivation and Performance," *Journal of Personality and Social Psychology* Volume 75, Issue 1 (1998). Pages 33-52.

2. H. G. Halvorson, "The Trouble With Bright Kids," *Harvard Business Review*, November 28, 2011, https://hbr .org/2011/11/the-trouble-with-bright-kids/.

3. J. E. Glaser, "Your Brain Is Hooked on Being Right," *Harvard Business Review,* February 23, 2013, https:// hbr.org/2013/02/break-your-addiction-to-being/.

4. T. Shahar, "Learn to Fail or Fail to Learn" (presented at the Mind and Its Potential Conference, Sydney, Australia, November 18-19, 2010).

5. M. Lewis, 'The No-Stats All-Star," *New York Times*, February 13, 2009, http://www.nytimes.com/2009/02/15/ magazine/15Battier-t.html?pagewanted=all&_r=0

6. William Shakespeare, *Henry VI,* Part III (Act II, Scene I, Line 85).

7. B. Brown, *Daring Greatly* (New York: Random House, 2012).

8. E. Ries, *The Lean Startup* (New York: Crown Business, 2011). Page 38.

9. E. Ries, *The Lean Startup* (New York: Crown Business, 2011). Page 49.

10. A. Tugend, "Winners Never Quit? Well, Yes, They Do," August 15, 2008, http://www.nytimes.com/2008/08/16/ business/16shortcuts.html?_r=3&ref=business&oref=s login&.

11. *Wikipedia*, "5 Whys," accessed March 19, 2015, http:// en.wikipedia.org/wiki/5_Whys.

Chapter 7

1. R. McGrath and I. MacMillan, "Discovery-Driven Planning," *Harvard Business Review,* July 1995, https://hbr .org/1995/07/discovery-driven-planning/ar/1.

2. *Wikipedia*, "Discovery Driven Planning," accessed March 19, 2015, http://en.wikipedia.org/wiki/Discovery -driven_planning.

3. D. Brooks, "It's Not About You," *New York Times,* May 30, 2011, http://www.nytimes.com/2011/05/31/ opinion/31brooks.html.

4. Korn Ferry, "Korn Ferry Survey: 87 Percent of Executives Want to Be CEO," October 2 2014, http://www.kornferry .com/press/korn-ferry-survey-87-percent-of-executives -want-to-be-ceo-yet-only-15-percent-of-execs-are -learning-agile-a-key-to-effective-leadership/.

5. A. Bhide, *The Origin and Evolution of New Businesses* (New York: Oxford University Press, 2000). Pages 207-215

6. L. E. McLeod, *Selling with Noble Purpose* (New York: Wiley, 2012). Page xv-xvi.

Afterword

1. B. Mandelbrot, *The (Mis)behavior of Markets* (New York: Basic Books, 2004). Pages 11-12.

References

Beck, Melinda. "Thank You. No, Thank You." *Wall Street Journal*, November 23, 2010. http://www.wsj.com/articles/SB10001424052748704243904575630541486290052.

Bednar, David A. "Bear Up Their Burdens with Ease." The Church of Jesus Christ of Latter-day Saints. April 2014. Accessed January 5, 2015. https://www.lds.org/general-conference/2014/04/bear-up-their-burdens-with-ease?lang=eng.

Bhide, Amar. *The Origin and Evolution of New Businesses*. New York: Oxford University Press, 2000.

Bienkowski, Sandra. "1-on1: Marcus Buckingham." *Success*, November 29, 2009. Accessed January 5, 2015. http://www.success.com/article/1-on-1-marcus-buckingham.

Brooks, David. "It's Not About You." *New York Times*, May 30, 2011. http://www.nytimes.com/2011/05/31/opinion/31brooks.html.

Brown, Brené. *Daring Greatly*. New York: Random House, 2012.

Bryant, Adam. "Conquering Your Fears of Giving Feedback." *New York Times*, December 29, 2012. Accessed January 5, 2015. http://www.nytimes.com/2012/12/30/business/karen-may-of-google-on-conquering-fears-of-giving-feedback.html?pagewanted=2.

Burnett, Mark, Clay Newbill, and Phil Gurin, executive producers. *Shark Tank,* Season 6, Episode 2. Aired on ABC September 26, 2014. Accessed October 30, 2014. http://abc.go.com/shows/shark-tank/episode-guide/season-06/602-season-6-premiere-roominate-wedding-wagon-floating-mug-and-kronos-golf.

Burroughs, Augusten. "Two-Minute Memoir: How to Ditch a Dream." *Psychology Today,* May 1, 2012. Accessed January 5, 2015. http://www.psychologytoday.com/articles/201206/two-minute-memoir-how-ditch-dream.

Carlile, Paul R., and Clayton M. Christensen. "The Cycle of Theory Building in Management Research." H*arvard Business Review,* July 5, 2006. http://hbswk.hbs.edu/item/5422.html.

Carson, Erin. "Vala Afshar: CMO. Writer. Twitter Storyteller. Future Restaurant Owner." *Tech Republic*, August 8, 2014. Accessed January 5, 2015. http://www.techrepublic.com/article/vala-afshar-cmo-writer-twitter-storyteller-future-restaurant-owner/.

Catalyst. *Percentage of Women Partners in Law Firms from 1995-2013 in the U.S., Select Years.* December 10, 2014. Accessed January 5, 2015, from http://www.catalyst.org/knowledge/percentage-women-partners-law-firms-1995-2013-us-select-years.

Chang, Kenneth. "Water Found on Moon, Researchers Say." *New York Times*, November 13, 2009. Accessed January 5, 2015. http://www.nytimes.com/2009/11/14/science/14moon.html?_r=1&.

Cherry, Elin. "The Unexpected and Wonderful Lessons of Being Fired." *Forbes,* January 22, 2015. http://www.forbes.com/sites/ellevate/2015/01/22/the-unexpected-and-wonderful-lessons-of-being-fired/.

Christensen, Clayton M. (1997). *The Innovator's Dilemma.* Cambridge, MA: Harvard Business School Press.

Christensen, Clayton M., James Allworth, and Karen Dillon. *How Will You Measure Your Life?* New York: HarperCollins, 2012.

Christensen, Clayton M., Richard Alton, Curtis Rising, and Andrew Waldeck. (2011, March). "The Big Idea: The New M&A Playbook." *Harvard Business Review,* March 2011. Accessed March 5, 2015. https://hbr.org/2011/03/the-big-idea-the-new-ma-playbook/ar/1.

Coyle, Daniel. (2013, January 7). "How to Get Better Feedback." *The Talent Code* blog, January 7, 2013. Accessed January 5, 2015.

Dugatkin, Lee Alan and Jean-Guy J. Godin. "Female Mating Preference for Bold Males in the Guppy *Poecilia reticulata.*" *Proceedings of the National Academy of Science of the United States of America* Volume 93 (1996): 10262–10267.

Dugatkin, Lee Alan. "The Evolution of Risk Taking." Dana Foundation, 2013, January 1, 2013. Accessed October 30, 2014. http://www.dana.org/cerebrum/default.aspx?id=39485.

Duhigg, Charles. *The Power of Habit.* New York: Random House, 2012.

Economist. "The Jobs Machine." *Economist,* April 13, 2013. http://www.economist.com/news/business/21576101-start-ups-founded-immigrants-are-creating-jobs-all-over-america-jobs-machine.

Entrepreneur magazine. "*Entrepreneur* Magazine's Hot 500." July 31, 2007. Accessed January 5, 2015. http://www.entrepreneur.com/article/181886.

Fasal Intuit. Fasal Intuit home page. Accessed January 5, 2015. http://fasal.intuit.com/.

Gladwell, Malcolm. *David and Goliath.* New York: Little, Brown and Company, 2013.

Glaser, Juduth E. "Your Brain Is Hooked on Being Right." *Harvard Business Review,* February 23, 2013. https://hbr.org/2013/02/break-your-addiction-to-being/.

Grush, Mary. "Blazing the Trail: Competency Based Education at SNHU." *Campus Technology*, December 13, 2013. Accessed January 5, 2015. http://campustechnology.com/articles/2013/12/18/competency-based-education-at-snhu.aspx.

Halvorson, Heidi Grant. "The Trouble with Bright Kids." *Harvard Business Review*, November 28, 2011. https://hbr.org/2011/11/the-trouble-with-bright-kids/.

Halvorson, Heidi Grant., and E. Tory Higgins. *Focus*. New York: Hudson Street Press, 2013.

Heffernan, Margaret. *Willful Blindness*. New York: Walker Publishing Company, 2010.

Hsu, Ming, Meghana Bhatt, Ralph Adolphs, Daniel Tranel, and Colin F. Camerer. "Neural Systems Responding to Degrees of Uncertainty in Human Decision-Making." *Science* Volume 310, Issue 5754 (2005): 1680–1683.

Hylton, Wil S. "The Unbreakable Laura Hillenbrand." *New York Times*, December 18, 2014. Accessed January 5, 2015. http://www.nytimes.com/2014/12/21/magazine/the-unbreakable-laura-hillenbrand.html?_r=0.

Iansiti, Marco, and Roy Levien. "Strategy for Small Fish." Harvard Business School, August 23, 2004. Accessed March 19, 2015. http://hbswk.hbs.edu/item/4331.html.

Isen, Alice M. "Missing in Action in the AIM: Positive Affects Facilitation of Cognitive Flexibility, Innovation and Problem Solving." *Psychological Inquiry* Volume 13, Issue 1(2002): 57–65.

Johansson, Frans. *The Click Moment*. New York: Penguin, 2012.

Johnson, Whitney. "How to Identify Your Disruptive Skills." *Harvard Business Review*, October 4, 2010. Accessed January 5, 2015. https://hbr.org/2010/10/how-to-identify-your-disruptiv.

Johnson, Whitney. *Harvard Business Review*, January 11, 2011. Accessed October 30, 2014. http://blogs.hbr.org/2011/01/thank-you-for-doing-your-job/.

Johnson, Whitney. "Rebecca Jackson: Under the Skin." *Whitney Johnson* blog, September 11, 2012. http://whitney johnson.com/rebecca-jackson-under-the-skin/.

Johnson, Whitney. "Throw Your Life a Curve." *Harvard Business Review*, September 3, 2012. Accessed March 5, 2015. https://hbr.org/2012/09/throw-your-life-a-curve/.

Johnson, Whitney. (2014, February 7). *Digging Deeper, Yahoo is Still Being Disrupted*. Accessed from Linkedin: https://www.linkedin.com/pulse/20140207144449 -3414257-digging-deeper-yahoo-the-disrupter-is-being -disrupted

Johnson, Whitney. "Disrupt Yourself." *Harvard Business Review*, September 1, 2014.

Johnson, Whitney. "To Innovate in a Big Company, Don't Think 'Us Against Them.'" *Harvard Business Review*, September 23, 2014. https://hbr.org/2014/09/to-innovate-in-a -big-company-dont-think-us-against-them/.

Kaplan, Saul. "How not to get 'Netflixed.'" *Fortune* magazine, October 11, 2011.

Kaufman, Scott Barry. "Does Creativity Require Constraints?" *Psychology Today*, August 30, 2011. Accessed March 7, 2015. https://www.psychologytoday.com/blog/beautiful-minds/201108/does-creativity-require -constraints.

Kirk, Mark, writer, director, producer. "The Warning." *Frontline*. Aired on Public Broadcast System, October 20, 2009. http://www.pbs.org/wgbh/pages/frontline/warning/.

Korn Ferry. "Korn Ferry Survey: 87 Percent of Executives Want to Be CEO." October 2, 2014. http://www.kornferry .com/press/korn-ferry-survey-87-percent-of-executives

-want-to-be-ceo-yet-only-15-percent-of-execs-are-learning-agile-a-key-to-effective-leadership/.

Lambie, Ryan. "The Production Nightmares That Made Jaws a Classic." Den of Geek, September 5, 2012. Accessed January 5, 2015. http://www.denofgeek.com/movies/22547/the-production-nightmares-that-made-jaws-a-classic.

Loukides, Mike. "The Revolution in Biology Is Here, Now." *O'Reilly Radar* blog, December 9, 2014. Accessed March 15, 2015. http://radar.oreilly.com/2014/12/the-revolution-in-biology-is-here-now.html.

Mandelbrot, Benoit. *The (Mis)behavior of Markets*. New York: Basic Books, 2004.

McGrath, Rita, and Ian MacMillan. "Discovery-Driven Planning." *Harvard Business Review*, July 1995. https://hbr.org/1995/07/discovery-driven-planning/ar/1.

McLeod, Lisa E. *Selling with Noble Purpose*. New York: Wiley, 2012.

Mendez, Juan Carlos. "S-Curve Model for Facebook and Dropbox User Adoption." *Juan Carlos Mendez* blog, August 21, 2012. Accessed March 5, 2015. http://jcmendez.info/2012/08/21/s-curve-model-for-facebook-and-dropbox-user-adoption.html.

Morgan, Adam, and Mark Barden. *A Beautiful Constraint*. Hoboken, New Jersey: John Wiley & Sons, 2015.

Mueller, Claudia M., and Carol S. Dweck. "Praise for Intelligence Can Undermine Children's Motivation and Performance." *Journal of Personality and Social Psychology* Volume 75, Issue 1 (1998): 33–52.

Nunes, Paul, and Tim Breene. *Jumping the S-Curve*. Boston: Harvard Business Review Press, 2011.

Oney, Steve. "The Defiant Ones." *Wall Street Journal*, November 12, 2010. Accessed January 5, 2015. http://www.wsj.com/articles/SB10001424052748703514904575602540345409292.

Pascual-Leone, Alvaro, Amir Amedi, Felipe Fregni, and Lotfi B. Merabet. "The Plastic Human Brain Cortex." *Annual Review of Neuroscience* Volume 28 (2005): 377–401.

Piff, Paul K. "Wealth and the Inflated Self." *Personality and Social Psychology Bulletin* (2013, December 19): 34–49.

Pipher, Mary. *Writing to Change the World*. New York: Riverhead Books, 2006.

Rangaswami, JP. "Thinking More About Twitter, Chatter and Knowledge Worker Pheromones." *Confused of Calcutta* blog, April 24, 2011. Accessed October 30, 2014. http://confusedofcalcutta.com/2011/04/24/thinking-more-about-twitter-chatter-and-knowledge-worker-pheromones/.

Rauch, Doug. "Failure Chronicles." *Harvard Business Review,* April 2011. https://hbr.org/2011/04/failure-chronicles/sb7.

Ries, Eric. *The Lean Startup*, New York: Crown Business, 2011

Rollins, Pam. Fox *42 Rules for Your New Leadership Role.* Super Star Press, 2011.

Scarlett, Joe. Joe Scarlett.com. Keynote at TN Governor's Conference for Economic Development accessed March 19, 2015. http://joescarlett.com/videos.html.

Schein, Edgar H. *Humble Inquiry.* San Francisco: Berrett-Koehler Publishers, 2013.

Shahar, Tal Ben. "Learn to Fail or Fail to Learn." Presented at the Mind and Its Potential Conference, Sydney, Australia, 2010.

Sheldon, Kennon M., Richard M. Ryan, Laird J. Rawsthorne, and Barbara Ilardi. "Trait Self and True Self: Cross-Role Variation in the Big Five Personality Traits with Psychological Authenticity and Subjective Well-Being." *Journal of Personal and Social Psychology* Volume 73, Issue 6 (1997): 1380–1391.

Simmons, Michael. "The No.1 Predictor of Career Success According to Network Science." *Forbes,* January 15,

2015. http://www.forbes.com/sites/michaelsimmons/2015/01/15/this-is-the-1-predictor-of-career-success-according-to-network-science/.

Skinner, Chris. "mBank: The World's First Mobile Social Bank within a Bank." *Financial Services Club Blog*, June 19, 2013. http://thefinanser.co.uk/fsclub/2013/06/mbank-the-worlds-first-mobile-social-bank-within-a-bank.html.

Starecheski, Laura. "This Is Your Stressed-Out Brain on Scarcity." National Public Radio *Shots* blog, July 14, 2014. Accessed March 7, 2015. http://www.npr.org/blogs/health/2014/07/14/330434597/this-is-your-stressed-out-brain-on-scarcity.

Sturt, David. *Great Work*. New York: McGraw-Hill, 2014.

Tierney, John. "A Serving of Gratitude May Save the Day." *New York Times*, November 21, 2011. http://www.nytimes.com/2011/11/22/science/a-serving-of-gratitude-brings-healthy-dividends.html?_r=1.

Tuttle, Dave. "Cortisol." *Life Extension Magazine*, July 2004. Accessed October 30, 2014, http://www.lef.org/magazine/2004/7/report_cortisol/Page-01.

Twenge, Jean M, and Joshua D. Foster. "Birth Cohort Increases in Narcissistic Personality Traits Among American College Students, 1982-2009." *Social Psychology and Personality Science* Volume 1, Issue 1(2010):99-106.

Ulwick, Anthony W. "Turn Customer Input into Innovation." *Harvard Business Review*, March 4, 2002.

Uzzi, Brian, Satyam Mukherjee, Michael Stringer, and Ben Jones. "Atypical Combinations and Scientific Impact." *Science* Volume 342, Issue 6257 (2013): 468–472.

Vorhauser-Smith, Sylvia. *The Neuroscience of Learning and Development*. Page Up People, March 19, 2015. http://www.pageuppeople.com/wp-content/uploads/2012/06/Neuroscience-of-Learning-and-Development1.pdf.

Wikipedia. "5 Whys." Accessed March 19, 2015. http://en.wikipedia.org/wiki/5_Whys.

Wikipedia. "Discovery Driven Planning." Accessed March 19, 2015, http://en.wikipedia.org/wiki/Discovery-driven_planning.

Wilson, David S., Kristine Coleman, Anne B. Clark, and Laurence Biederman. "Shy-Bold Continuum in Pumpkinseed Sunfish (Lepomis gibbosus): An Ecological Study of a Psychological Trait." *Journal of Comparative Psychology Volume* 107, Issue 3 (1993): 250–260.

Wilson, David S., Anne B. Clark, Kristine Coleman, and Ted Dearstyne. "Shyness and Boldness in Humans and Other Animals." *Trends in Ecology and Evolution* Volume 9, Issue 11, (1994): 442–446.

Wiltbank, Robert. "Robert Wiltbank." Willamette University, March 19, 2015. http://www.willamette.edu/~wiltbank/seattle_angel_conference_may_2012.html.

Wiseman, Liz. "Why Your Team Needs Rookies." *Harvard Business Review,* October 2, 2014. https://hbr.org/2014/10/why-your-team-needs-rookies.

World Bank. *World Development Report 2015 Explores "Mind, Society, and Behavior."* World Bank, December 2, 2014. Accessed March 7, 2015. http://www.worldbank.org/en/news/feature/2014/12/02/world-development-report-2015-explores-mind-society-and-behavior.

Index

About the Author

WHITNEY JOHNSON is an investor, speaker, author, and leading thinker on driving corporate innovation through personal disruption. Johnson co-founded the investment firm Rose Park Advisors along with Clayton Christensen where they led the seed round for Korea's Coupang. Having served as president from 2007 to 2012, Johnson was involved in fund formation, capital raising, and the development of the fund's strategy. During her tenure, the CAGR of the Fund was 11.98 percent versus 1.22 percent for the S&P 500.

Previously, Johnson was an *Institutional Investor*-ranked analyst for eight consecutive years, and was rated by Starmine as a superior stock-picker. As an equity analyst, Ms. Johnson's stocks under coverage included America Movil (NYSE: AMX), Televisa (NYSE: TV), and Telmex (NYSE: TMX), which accounted for roughly 40 percent of Mexico's stock exchange.

Johnson is a frequent contributor and writer, including to the *Harvard Business Review*, as a LinkedINfluencer, and through other channels. She is the author of *Disrupt Yourself: Putting the Power of Disruptive Innovation to Work* and *Dare, Dream, Do: Remarkable Things Happen When You Dare to Dream* (Bibliomotion: 2012). She is also a prolific speaker and has spoken to audiences of more than 30,000 on her ideas and vision. Johnson is represented by the New Leaf Speakers bureau, along with other thought leaders in innovation like Steve Wozniak.

Johnson has received widespread recognition for her work and ideas and was named one of Fortune's 55 Most Influential Women On Twitter in 2014. She was named a finalist in the Future Thinker Award for Management Thinkers50, as well as fellow at the Tribeca Disruptive Innovation Awards. She co-founded the popular Forty Women Over Forty to Watch. Johnson and her work have been covered in *The Atlantic, BBC, CNN, Fast Company, The Guardian, Harvard Business Review, The Wall Street Journal,* and more.

For more on personal disruption, look up whitney-johnson.com/disruptyourself. For more on her latest thinking, including tips on disruption, sign up for her newsletter at whitneyjohnson.com. To book for speaking, contact johnson@newleafspeakers.com, to hire her as an advisor, contact whitney@whitneyjohnson.com, and for bulk book purchases, alicia@bibliomotion.com.

Presenting the Disrupt Yourself™ KEYNOTE

Consider this simple yet powerful idea: disruptive companies and ideas upend markets by doing something truly different—they see a need, an empty space waiting to be filled, and they dare to create something for which a market may not yet exist. As president and co-founder of Rose Park Advisors' Disruptive Innovation Fund with Clayton Christensen, Whitney Johnson utilized the theory of disruptive innovation to invest in publicly traded stocks and private early stage companies.

As Whitney immersed herself in applying the frameworks of disruption to innovation and investing, she discovered the theory also applies to individuals, and that the S-curve model we use to gauge how quickly an innovation will be adopted, can also help us understand the psychology of personal disruption. In her keynote, she provides a fresh perspective on innovation and change, identifying seven variables, that can slow up or speed down movement along the S-curve, including taking the right kinds of risk, battling entitlement, and being driven by discovery.

This speech is for YOU if you are:

- a high potential individual charting your career trajectory
- a leader trying to jumpstart innovative thinking in your company
- a self-starter ready to make a disruptive pivot in your business

This speech is for your COMPANY if:

- revenue growth is peaking and you need to reinvent
- innovative thinking among your management team has stalled
- industry changes are making the future uncertain

We are living in an era of accelerating disruption—as you manage the S-curve waves of learning and mastering you will not only cope, but harness the power and unpredictability of disruption to catapult you forward. If you want to be successful in unexpected ways, follow your own disruptive path. Dare to innovate. Do something astonishing. Disrupt yourself™.

To book Whitney, contact New Leaf Speakers, johnson@newleafspeakers.com, (781) 797-0440

MAR - - 2016